A MANUAL
OF CHRISTIAN BELIEFS

A MANUAL
OF CHRISTIAN BELIEFS

BY

EDWIN LEWIS

PROFESSOR OF SYSTEMATIC THEOLOGY IN DREW THEOLOGICAL SEMINARY
AUTHOR OF "JESUS CHRIST AND THE HUMAN QUEST"

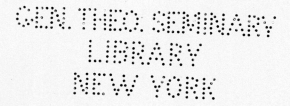
NEW YORK
CHARLES SCRIBNER'S SONS
1927

PREFACE

This book has had its origin very largely in informal discussions with various groups of men and women on subjects connected with the Christian religion. It has been my privilege for several years past to conduct such discussions in open forums and conferences, the members of which represented a considerable range of culture and a wide variety of religious affiliations. These discussions have revealed at once a deep interest in the subject of Christian belief and an astonishing vagueness and uncertainty concerning it. I have had ample evidence that the positions here set forth have proved helpful to minds perplexed as to what Christianity as a system of belief is, and as to what it implies.

The implications are, in a way, as important as the substance. This is why a certain amount of philosophical background has been introduced, especially in the consideration of the nature of God and of the problem of evil and sin. It is possible to simplify Christianity too much. "The simple Gospel" turns out, on consideration, to involve a theory of things which is as radical and challenging and far-reaching as anything we can conceive. "Even thinking is divine service," and it is no denial of the emotional elements of Christianity to attempt to justify it at the bar of reason.

In the appendices, references are given to a limited amount of relevant literature. There are also suggested topics for further discussion, and lists of questions for each chapter that will serve the student for purposes of review.

EDWIN LEWIS.

Drew Forest,
    Madison, New Jersey,
        April 18, 1927.

CONTENTS

CONTENTS

A MANUAL
OF CHRISTIAN BELIEFS

A MANUAL OF CHRISTIAN BELIEFS

INTRODUCTION

The bewildering rapidity with which science in recent years has brought to light new facts about the world and about human life has not been without its effect on the Christian religion and certain of its distinctive beliefs. What once seemed to be so secure has come to be called in question, and there is a wide-spread uneasiness even among Christian people themselves. Christianity was promulgated in the first place, and its distinctive doctrines were wrought out, at a time when the view of the world was radically different from what it is to-day. Although much has been done to rehabilitate Christianity from the modern point of view, it cannot yet be said that the effort has been entirely successful. Indeed, it is a question in the mind of many whether it can be done at all without surrendering so much that what is left will not be Christianity in any recognizable sense.

There are many who believe that the only way out of the difficulty is by distinguishing between Christianity as a religion of experience and Christianity as a system of belief. They claim that what is fundamental is the way of living, and perhaps also the way of feeling, but that the way of thinking is secondary and incidental. A little reflection will show that while such a distinction may have a certain practical value, it is impossible to make the distinction absolute. While it may be true that there are beliefs formerly insisted upon by the entire church which may be surrendered without imperilling the Christian way of life, such as, for example, the literal inerrancy of Scripture, the passing of the guilt of Adam upon all his descendants, and the penal character of the sufferings of Christ, it is equally true that no man will endeavor to live the Christian way who does not accept certain beliefs. He will at least believe that the Christian way is the best way to live, and he will soon find, if he considers the matter, that that single belief commits him to a great many other beliefs as well.

And it is just as true that there cannot be the inward Christian experience without certain associated ideas. There are those who propose to sever Christianity altogether from questions of behavior and questions of belief, and to reduce it to a form of mysticism, a sense of inward peace and calm, a consciousness of harmony with God. But even in so-called feeling we both act and think. An "inner experience" is, after all, a form of personal behavior, in the sense that we are consciously participating in something, and it is also in part the result of what we believe or think or hope.

It is impossible therefore to eliminate from Christianity a thought element. There never has been and there never will be a religion that is entirely non-theological or non-doctrinal. This does not mean that the theology and the doctrine are to be made everything, but it does mean that they are highly important, and in a sense indispensable. The church exists to help make the world Christian, and it is to do that by teaching certain facts, certain ideas, certain beliefs. If these facts, ideas, and beliefs are not true, the church has no good reason for its existence. If they are true, then the task of the church becomes at once clearly defined and imperative.

The question therefore concerns these facts, ideas, and beliefs, as to what they are, and whether they are true. The question involves a threefold appeal—the appeal to history, to experience, and to reason. In making that appeal, we find we are justified in discriminating between what is fundamental in Christianity and what is not. There is probably no one who could to-day assent to all that at one time or another has been put forward as a part of Christianity. The history of Christian thought reveals a process of taking on and of laying off. But there is always a vital core of truth to which the additions have been made, and which men have been determined to preserve when the alleged additions began to fall under suspicion.

This is the situation to-day. There is a body of fact and belief which is essential to the continuity of the Christian religion. Perhaps no two men would agree precisely as to what this is. What some regard as fundamental, others regard as incidental. But there is, nevertheless, a large area of belief which Christian people have always shared in common. In the following pages an attempt is made to set forth this common truth, and to state some of the reasons which justify its imperial claims. The introduction here and there of philosophical positions is simply for the sake of providing an undercurrent of intellectual continuity.

I

THE EXISTENCE AND THE ACTIVITY OF GOD

(1) *God Himself*

All religion is bound up with the conviction that there is a Power with which human life is inextricably involved, and that the proper understanding of this Power, and the proper relation to it, are indispensable to the highest human well-being. Under some form or another, this Power is what is meant by God. Both the personal and the social worth of the religion are determined by the way in which the Power is regarded. A religion can never be greater than its God. What we regard as the debasing features of religious history are the direct or indirect result of the way in which the God is understood.

The Nature of God. Because God means different things to different people, it is necessary that we give the term some definition before we proceed to ask if it represents a reality. With a few exceptions, God has always meant, in religion, one who knows that he exists and what he is doing. If God is reduced to the blind Fate of the Greek, or to the Heaven of the Confucianist, or to the Natural Law of the materialist, or to the Ideal Humanity of the humanist, certain of the most distinctive features of religion, especially those of fellowship and communion, become impossible. Religion means a good deal more than awe in the presence of the impersonal, or patient submission to fate, or self-sur-

6

render to an ideal, or enthusiastic devotion to social betterment.

What then do we mean by "God Himself"? Speaking at present in the most general terms, we mean a self-conscious Being whose life never began and will never end; but for whom there would be nothing else; upon whom therefore all else depends; and of whom therefore all else will be to some extent a self-revelation. What is the evidence that such a Being exists? Would he still exist even if we did not? If there are other intelligences who know God, by our definition they would necessarily issue from God himself. He could not be known unless there were those who could know him, but his existence is presupposed in the knowledge because his existence is presupposed in the knower.

The Fact of Creation. Most people are agreed that we do not make the world, but find it. Some have argued to the contrary, but the argument is not convincing. There is a "given" element in our experience. Knowledge is always a knowledge *of*. The question as to what the world may be like apart from how we know it is not only a purely academic question: for the ordinary man, it creates an unnecessary confusion of thought. Our world is the world as we know it, and that is the only world in which we can have any vital interest. Nevertheless, because we know, there is something that we know which in a measure is independent of our knowing.

This independent aspect of the world is one reason for believing in God. We want to account for that which our minds do not make but find, and we account for it as due to the activity of another mind. There are, of course, those who say that this is not necessary. They would have us stop with what we "find," and regard this as self-existent and self-explaining. The difficulties of this view will appear in a moment. It suffices to say here that it is a question of choosing between two alternatives. The world speaks to us. Does it speak to us entirely on its own account, as a mere impersonal system; or does it speak to us because it is itself the utterance of an Infinite Intelligence?

The Nature of Man. We cannot leave out of creation the human self that knows it and that understands and appreciates it. The mind in which creation reflects itself is itself a part of creation. If we need God to account for the known, much more do we need him to account for the knower.

There are those who suppose that since the evolutionary hypothesis explains man as a product of nature, man no longer presupposes God. But a process is not explained merely by being described. If man is a child of nature, then nature must be so conceived as to be able to account for the offspring. None of our theories about man can make him any other than he is. He is a rational and ethical being, no matter how he came to be that. It is true that his life is closely interwoven with the life of the world. Evolution means that man is embedded in nature. That being so, we have to do one of two things: either say that man's rational and ethical nature is a product of forces which are neither rational nor ethical, and this is incredible; or say that these natural forces are the instruments of a higher rational and ethical Being who uses them to produce other beings like unto himself.

The Moral Imperative. The significance of man's ethical nature in this connection cannot be emphasized too strongly. Man can never quite escape "the sense of the ought." It does not matter in the least what theory we may hold as to the process whereby he comes to believe that certain things are right and ought to be done, and that certain things are wrong and ought not to be done. Nor does it matter that the ideas of right and wrong have varied so immensely from time to time. Man has an ethical history, and he could not have that unless already he had ethical capacity. All education presupposes the educatee. Man is continually increasing his knowledge of nature and his control over it; that is because he is a rational being. But he is also continually seeking the "better"—a better way to live, a better way to be, a better way to use his acquisitions. That very search for a better implies the recognition of a difference between what actually is and what ought to be.

The power to recognize that difference is an inseparable part of human nature. Take it entirely away, and what is left would not be what we mean by human. We cannot define man fully without including his moral capacity. The moral that characterizes man must therefore be traced to the forces that produce man—unless, indeed, we are to commit the fallacy of accounting for the greater by the lesser. In a word, because man is rational, the source of his being is rational. Because he is ethical, the source of his being is ethical. Rational and ethical man presupposes a rational and ethical God.

Religious Experience. Man is not only rational and ethical: he is religious as well. One could live according to reason, and not be religious. One could observe the strictest ethical code, and not be religious. A distinctive feature of historical religion has always been its supernatural reference. Religion involves belief in some sort of Deity, and men have taken the ensuing experience as indubitable evidence that the belief is true.

Those who wish to do so may say that religious experience is due to a false belief in the first place. There is no God: consequently religious experience is self-delusion. Perhaps that is so; but then, again, *perhaps that is not so.* Precisely there lies the crux of the whole situation. The evidential value of religious experience has weight only for those who have the experience, and the experience is necessarily conditioned on faith. "He that cometh to God must believe that he is." Personal fellowship with his God, which to the worshipper is all-sufficient, is meaningless to the sceptical observer.

The precondition to religious experience therefore is faith. Can such faith be vindicated? Is it rational to "believe where we cannot prove"? The test, provided the object of faith is not inherently incredible, must be a practical one—*fruits.* Much evil has been done in the name of religious faith, but that proves nothing, any more than the evil done in the name of love destroys the worth of love. Self-sacrifice, not lust, is the real measure of love; and its good works, not its evil, is the real measure of religious faith. One has only to take out of the world to-day, and out of human life, all that is there because men believe in God, to realize how fruitful a principle faith is.

Revelation. According to what has now been said, the fact of creation, the fact of man as a rational and ethical being, and the fact of religious experience, all bear witness to God. In one way or another, they involve the divine activity, and they are therefore to be considered as forms of divine revelation. In these various ways, God is making himself known. He is showing what kind of God he is.

This general revelation does not preclude the possibility of a more special revelation. Because we are in contact with God everywhere does not mean that we may understand him just as fully through one fact as through another. It rather creates the probability that we shall see him more clearly in some events than in others. Experience supports this antecedent probability. There are certain incidents, certain historic movements, certain personalities, even certain writings through which we believe that most of all we find God. Where we most fully find God, he is most fully active, and therefore most fully revealed. Where is this fuller revelation found? In great and good men. Goodness is Godlikeness. Where there is most of goodness, there is most of God. In a perfectly good man God would himself be perfectly revealed.

(2) *God and the World*

God Completely Separate from the World. It is possible to think of God and the world as standing over against each other in complete separation. The two are related merely as a workman and his work. The world is something that God made, but he lives his life apart from it. He was perfect before he made it; he is perfect apart from it, even although it now exists; and he would still be perfect if it should entirely pass away.

From this standpoint, there are two ways of accounting for the world: (1) God made the world out of some kind of raw material which existed from all eternity. God himself never began to be, and the stuff ("matter") out of which he made the world never began to be. There was therefore always the possibility of a universe, but the conversion of the possibility into a reality had to wait on God's will. He began his task when he chose to begin it, using material that already lay to his hand. There are those who believe that Genesis 1:2

teaches this view that God formed or shaped the world out of material already existing. (2) God made the world out of nothing by the sheer exercise of his creative will. The view supposes that there was a time when God alone existed, and there was nothing else. All he needed to do to have a universe was to will to have one, and it forthwith appeared. If he should will to have it no longer, it would instantly cease to be. This act of creation "out of nothing" is held to be the prerogative of God, since he is omnipotent, and can do whatever he wills to do.

The first theory is at least conceivable, although its difficulties have been greatly increased by the modern discovery that all matter is energy. It would therefore require us to believe that there is an eternal energy other than God. How two eternal energies could be completely independent of one another does not appear. The second theory breaks on the maxim which most people feel to be indisputable: "Out of nothing, nothing is made." It is possible, of course, to regard the world as a mere mental panorama, a picture that we imagine, and one that exists only in our minds. But the imagining mind would still have to be accounted for. That, at least, exists now, and once did not. Then whence came it? Was it also made "out of nothing"? The question simply suggests the difficulty of any view which entirely separates the Creator and the created.

God's Complete Identity with the World. At the other extreme from the view just considered is the view that God and the universe are one and the same. This is Pantheism. All separate existences in their totality give us God.

Many believe that this view is really a denial of God altogether. Indeed, a modern exponent of it has said quite frankly: "Pantheism is a polite way of saying that there is no God." Moreover, the view makes human life merely a passing phase of the life of the whole, as the wave is a temporary disturbance of the ocean but nothing different from it. It destroys any essential differences as between the divine, the human, and the non-human. Certainly, so far as religion is concerned, the distinction between the human and the divine is taken for granted; and while pantheists have often been deeply religious, it would seem that their religion was *in spite of* and not *because of* their peculiar belief.

God and the World in Organic Relation. There is a third view which regards the world not as wholly detached from God, nor as wholly identical with him, but as a form under which he manifests himself. The world could have no existence apart from God, but he is not it, and it is not he. It exists because he also exists, but its existence is in the fact that it is a form of his activity. We may adopt this view, and still regard the world as having a reality of its own, and moving forward in obedience to dependable laws. But it will also follow that we are everywhere in touch with God, that the laws of nature are the laws of God, and that the more completely we understand and appreciate nature, the more completely we understand and appreciate God.

This view assumes that God is eternally creative. God is creative because he is active. We cannot think of him not being active; therefore we cannot think of a time when there was not something else besides him. This does not mean that the present form of the divine creative action is eternal, but only that the present is always continuous with the past. We can never find, nor can we ever think, an absolute beginning—that is, a form of existence prior to which there was nothing.

This, of course, involves the whole problem of what we mean by "time" and "eternity," a problem too difficult for a discussion like the present. It must suffice to say that God is forever active, and that he is himself necessarily present in his own activity, and that therefore between God and his activity there is a vital relationship which we can best describe by the word organic.

God Within and Without the World. Many problems go with the view just described, in particular the problems of natural evil, of personal self-consciousness, of freedom, and of sin. These problems would be quite insoluble if all that we could say about God was that he indwelt the world, the immanent sustainer of its life.

We must also regard him as transcending it. He is within the world, but he is also without it. These terms are not to be regarded merely as terms of location. When we say that God transcends the world, we mean that the world at any given time does not exhaust all his power or reveal all his life. There is always, so to speak, a divine "plus," a divine reserve. God has therefore never spoken his last word; he has never done all he purposes to do. What he says or does at a given time is always part of a larger whole, and is to be understood accordingly. There is yet more light to break forth, and as it comes it will illuminate what before was dark.

Meanwhile we exercise faith. It is because God is transcendent that faith is rational. There is a form of the divine activity which we know by observation and direct experience, and to that extent we know God also. But that is not sufficient. There is a knowledge of God that is born of faith and trust. Faith lays hold of God in other aspects of his being than those which nature makes known. The transcendent God reveals himself to faith as the immanent God reveals himself to rational processes. We come thereby to an increasing certainty that there actually is in God that love, that holiness, and that grace to which, in greater or lesser degree, religious experience has always borne its testimony.

II

THE CHRISTIAN CONCEPTION OF GOD

Men may believe in God either through philosophy or through religion. They may be prompted either by the needs of the reason or by the needs of the heart. There is no necessary antagonism between the two, yet it is possible to place the emphasis on one side rather than on the other. Some men want God as the explanation of a problem; others want him as the satisfaction of a deep moral need. In Christianity we have a conception of God that does both.

The Christian God and the Religious Need. The Christian conception of God is concerned primarily with the emotional and ethical need. This is seen finally to be a vital factor in giving it its intellectual strength and completeness. We can think of our life both as to the *fact* of it and as to the *meaning* of it. We need a God who can not only account for the fact, but who can also explain the meaning.

Frail though we are in many ways, we are bigger than the world we live in. We can ask the world questions it cannot answer. We have needs that the world cannot satisfy. We have powers that the world cannot call into action. Religion has to do with these facts. It assumes that we are more than we seem to be, and that the world is more than it seems to be.

Christianity claims to interpret to us this "more." It recognizes in us powers and capacities by virtue of which we are the children of God. It sees the world as the place in which we are to realize and express our son-

16

ship. And it sees in God one whose sole concern is with his children's good, one who conducts the world with that end in view, and one who will stop short of nothing that is possible to him as he pursues his purpose of good.

A Purposive God. Christianity believes in a God who has a gracious purpose which determines all his dealings with men. It regards the world as an instrument of this purpose, created and sustained by the God who thus employs it. Human life is not simply the closing stage of a vast mechanical evolutionary process, which began in death and will end in death. Rather is it human life that gives its significance to everything else. God's primary concern is not with the mechanics of the universe, with its bulk, its distances, its magnitudes, but with the human life which the universe makes possible. It is only to men that God can speak. The divine purpose is therefore to be understood in the light of what human life can do and be.

This view gives a perfectly free hand to science in its investigations of the universe, but it at the same time claims that the scientific findings are limited in their application. The physical conditions to life, the age of the earth, the distances of the stars, the probability of life on the earth finally becoming extinct—all these are legitimate subjects of scientific research. Instead of minimizing the significance of human life, however, such research only enhances it. To the man who construes the divine purpose through the needs and capacities of human life, and who sees in the universe the divinely constructed stage on which the first act of the endless drama of that life is to be played—to such a man, the more wonderful the stage is made to appear, the more impressive becomes the value of what is being enacted on it. "The play's the thing." For Christian thought,

God's purpose is primarily with men, to bring them by means of their manifold contacts with the world to intimate personal fellowship with himself.

A Fatherly God.   Christianity, understanding God's purpose with reference to what man is able to be, interprets that ability in terms of sonship and brotherhood. It teaches both that man is *able* to be filial in his attitude toward God, and fraternal in his attitude toward his fellows, and that he is *intended* so to be. This is why God made him in the first place. This is why God surrounds him with such conditions as he does. In so far, therefore, as a man refuses to do this, he challenges the divine purpose, and he writes failure over his own life. The possibility of this refusal is always present. No man can be coerced into sonship and brotherhood. He has the power to be a son, and he has the power to be a brother, but the same power that may issue in the filial and the fraternal may also issue in hostility and indifference.

It is because Christianity thus understands the divine purpose that it speaks of God as a Father. There are undoubtedly aspects of the divine nature to which the term Father is hardly applicable. But religion is not directly concerned with these. It is concerned with God in that aspect of him in which he is knowable to men and may enter into intimate personal relations with them. So considered, God is to Christian thought a Father. The laws of life as they affect men are the laws of a Father. The severities of life are a Father's severities. The joys that life makes possible are such as a Father could wish his children to have, and joys that the Father cannot approve are not worthy of the children. The experiences that seem hard to endure and to understand are so many opportunities for the filial spirit to come to self-assertion, and by the assertion to become more sure of itself and more sure of God the Father. God would have men become one great family; he has made man so that this is possible; and he is such a God as can have this for his purpose and as can do whatever is necessary to carry it out.

An Approachable God. For Christian thought, then, there is possible between God and man the most intimate personal relationship. This does not mean that God is in any way cheapened, or that there is an ignoring of his majesty and power. There is no incompatibility between thinking of God as the Source of the universe and God as the intimate Personal Companion of men. Although Christian thought, building on the Old Testament, and to some extent even on Greek philosophy, takes the divine creatorship more or less for granted, it does that because its point of view is consistently with the meaning of God for human life and experience. It believes that God is accessible to the weakest and most ignorant of his children, and that he finds satisfaction in the approach.

This experience of God by man may be direct and immediate. It may take place anywhere and under any circumstances, provided only that there may be the inward attitude of faith and love. This is not to deny the proper place to aids of various sorts. Any form or device is legitimate that makes God more real to men, or that makes men more sure of God, but it ceases to be legitimate the moment it becomes an end rather than a means. God is not far off, but near. "A present help is he." He is as close to us as we are to ourselves. He is beyond, but it is "a beyond that is within." It is not the wise of head but the pure in heart who find God. The God who can be approached *only* through another, or *only* through prescribed external forms, is not the Christian God. Not that we can know the *whole* truth of God by a direct experience of him. But what we *need* to know about him for the purposes of religious faith and for the realization of our sonship—this not only *may* be a direct personal discovery, but it *must* be. Christianity deals not with an inferential but with an experiential God. What it says about him are not mere suppositions, but verifiable certainties.

A Suffering God.   The Christian God is one whose purpose with men involves him in suffering. Here again we meet an aspect of God which can hardly be called for by philosophical reflection. Ordinarily, the God of philosophy has been one who was entirely undisturbed by the events of time. The Unknowable, the Uncondi-tioned, the Absolute—these are the terms under which philosophy has been wont to speak of God. Man, with all his varied needs, considers such a God as this, and he says very simply, *it is not enough.* He does not want a God merely to explain how things can be. He does not want a God of whom all he can say is that he is First Cause and Sustaining Power. He wants a God who is *interested* in the work of his own hands.

Christianity, following the Old Testament, claims that God has this interest, but it makes it a *costly* inter-est, an idea also suggested in the Old Testament, but not yet fully developed. It is costly because he regards men as his children, because he loves them as a Father, and because his greatest desire for them is that they shall be his worthy sons. His purpose with them can never be realized except they pass through the school of discipline, and God himself devises the discipline. But the purpose is a Father's purpose; the method is a Father's method; and the Father himself shares in the suffering which the purpose and the method require.

This is the Christian belief. It is easy enough to say that it rests on a false analogy of Divine Fatherhood with human fatherhood. It is easy enough to ask, "How can the Infinite and Eternal Being suffer?" If God were solitary, he would not suffer. He *chooses* to suffer because he chooses to make a world in which suffering is inevitable. His suffering, so far from detracting from his perfection, is an evidence of it. He is too great not to suffer. He has a personal interest in men, and for that reason he seeks their highest good. Ignorance, sin, error, and their various penalties cause suffering to God because they cause suffering to men. He is himself present in every redeeming and saving effort, by whomever made; and he is supremely present as the Suffering God in the sacrificial deed by which Jesus Christ finished his work.

A God of Holy Love. If we properly understood the word "love," it would suffice to say that God is a God of love. It is because God loves that he suffers. But his love is a holy love; or, better still, it is the love of one who is in his innermost nature holy, and there is always a danger that this holiness will be lost sight of. To regard God's love as mere benevolence or good-nature is to endanger such verities as the wrath of God and the certainty of the operation of the moral law.

In the case of men, there is often a discrepancy between love and holiness, but never in the case of God. God's holiness is his deep concern for what is *right*. His love is his deep concern for men's good. But the two are never in conflict. God sets himself against sin, and God punishes sin, not merely because he is a holy God, but also because he is a God of love. For him to make light of sin would be as much a violation of his love as of his holiness. The good that God in his love seeks for men is always a moral good. It is a dangerous thing to suppose that we can play with sin because God is love. Sin is the denial of his right to control us, and we make such a denial to our own hurt. We know that evil is evil because of the way it affects human life. But those effects are part of the moral order which God himself ordains. The moral order, both as restraining evil and as promoting good, is determined by God's own nature. His nature is therefore seen to be holy love because his purpose is that we shall find blessedness in and through righteousness.

An All-Sufficient God. Some will have missed in this discussion such terms as omnipotence, omnipresence, omniscience, absoluteness, self-existence, trinity, and so on. The difficulty with these terms is the profound disagreement as to their meaning. What, for example, is meant by saying that God can do everything and that he knows everything? The Christian religion is interested in God mainly as to his purpose with human life, and it believes that with respect to that purpose he is *utterly adequate.* For Christianity, the various philosophical terms just mentioned are of value chiefly as expressing this divine adequacy. God is in himself such a God that he can know and do whatever his purpose with men requires that he shall know and do. Men are forever being baffled, but God is never baffled. He never wills to know what he cannot know, or to do what he cannot do.

It is from this practical standpoint that we can best of all understand what is known as the Trinity. On the basis of the baptismal formula, the apostolic benediction, and the New Testament teaching about the divine sonship of Christ and about the Holy Spirit, later Christian thought constructed a highly speculative doctrine about the interior life of God, namely, that God necessarily and from eternity exists as three distinct persons in one. The great truth that underlies the speculation is just this truth of God's utter adequacy. That is to say, there is in God that which answers to every need of his purpose and to every need of men. His purpose calls for his revealing himself to men in a human life; men need such a revelation; in Jesus Christ that twofold need is met. Again, his purpose calls for his manifesting himself in the hearts and minds of men as a sanctifying and illuminating presence; men need to be so sanctified and illuminated; in the Holy Spirit that twofold need is met.

Fundamentally, therefore, the doctrine of the Trinity means that there is an inexhaustible capacity in God to meet every situation that is evoked by his purpose to impart himself to men in redeeming love and power. He would save men, and he is able to provide from within himself a Saviour. He would lead men into holiness of life, and as men seek this holiness he is able to associate himself with them as the Holy Spirit, or the Spirit of Holiness.

A God Seen in Christ. The primary source of the Christian idea of God is Jesus Christ. We must remember, however, that he came into the moral and religious heritage of the nation of which he was born. Not only so, but he inspired a great number of other men with the message he brought and the life he lived, and these men added something on their own account to what they had received from their Lord. The Christian idea of God, therefore, connects on the one hand with the God of the Hebrew people, especially as he came to be understood by their great prophets; and, on the other hand, with the stream of Christian thought throughout the centuries.

Nevertheless, it is with God as he was revealed in and by Jesus Christ that the Christian man is supremely concerned. This fact provides us with a standard whereby all that is said about God elsewhere may be measured. Much that is said about God in the Old Testament cannot be accepted by the Christian because it cannot be brought into agreement with the God who is revealed in Christ. This, of course, is only what we should expect in view of the fact that God's revelation of himself in history had to be gradual, according as men were able to receive and understand it. What is much more difficult to account for is the way in which non-Christian ideas of God have maintained themselves in Christian thought. Such assertions as that the sin of the first man makes all the rest of us guilty, and that the newly born babe is the object of God's wrath and could justly be punished forever, ought never to have been made by any man for whom "God was in Christ." This is not to say—as will be seen later—that there is no moral urgency in the Gospel, or that a belief in God's grace permits us to make light of sin. The Christian God is one who is required to account for the total fact of Christ, in all he was and said and did. Such a God, as we said before, will be all-holy, but he will also be all-loving. He will do nothing with men nor require anything from men which will violate either holiness or love, because he is "the Christlike God."

The process whereby the very and eternal God could be revealed in a human life has always challenged the Christian intellect. We do not have to agree as to the process before we can accept the fact. It suffices that we see in the character of Jesus Christ a perfect manifestation of the character of God. There are aspects of God's nature not revealed in Christ, and necessarily so. What is there revealed is what we need to know in order to be saved. We are saved according as we come to sonship and brotherhood. What that sonship and brotherhood is we learn in Jesus Christ. We therefore learn at the same time what God is: in respect to men he is as a Father, holy, loving, sacrificial, forgiving, redeeming. What Christ would do for men, God would do for men. What Christ would have men be, God would have men be. What Christ is, God is. We need nothing more.

III

MAN: BODY AND SPIRIT

We have said that the idea of God has both a religious interest and a philosophical interest. God may be considered either as the Causal Power which accounts for the universe as a fact; or as the Living Spirit who responds to certain imperishable needs in human nature. The religious interest is in God as a Living Spirit who makes himself known to men and who shares his life with them. The divine purpose with man—if there be such—will be expected to determine the nature of man, just as the nature of man will afford a clue as to the divine purpose. If God would impart himself to other creatures, those creatures must be such as shall be able to receive him. If, again, there are creatures who are able to receive God—able, that is, to think about him, to believe in him, to trust him, to have an experience which they account for as the realization of his presence with them—then this ability will, in its turn, reveal and illustrate the divine purpose. Briefly, an understanding of man will help to an understanding of God. Man's increasing self-realization will be at once an increasing realization of God's purpose and an increasing revelation of God's nature.

Man a Divine Creation. The Christian idea of man as a divine creation is derived largely from the Old Testament. "It is he that hath made us, and not we ourselves." This is the burden of the Scripture teaching, and a detailed collocation of that teaching would be simply so many different ways of stating this same truth. The Scriptures recognize the ordinary distinction of body and spirit, and they make God the Author of both. In the exercise of his Sovereign Will and Power, God, we are told, made all things, and he crowned his work with man. He breathed into man something of his own Spirit, and endued him with capacities like unto those he himself possessed. He set a limit to man's years, and he set a limit to man's powers, but within the limits of those years and powers he gave him dominion over all else.

Body and Spirit in the Scriptures. The Scriptures contain little theorizing about the relation of body and spirit. There is, indeed, both an Old Testament and a New Testament psychology, but our immediate purpose does not call for a detailed study of it. The Hebrews certainly regarded human life as a body and spirit unit, so much so that it was long before they developed a doctrine of the immortality of the soul. Even when they did develop it, they kept their feeling for the "wholeness" of life by developing in connection with it a doctrine of the resurrection of the body. The Sadducees' denial of resurrection represents only a minority view. In our Lord's time, the idea of demoniac possession was widespread. The essence of the idea was that the rightful occupant of the body was either subjected to the control of the evil spirit (Mark 9:17–26), or even entirely displaced (Matt. 12:43–45). Paul's teaching on "flesh" and "spirit" (Rom. 7:14–25; 8:1–17) may possibly mean that he finds the root of evil in the body, but it is more likely that he regards "flesh" and "spirit" as two antagonistic principles, to the first of which man is by nature subject, and to the second of which he may become subject by divine grace. Paul also speaks of "body, soul, and spirit" (1 Thess.

5 : 23), from which some infer that he recognized a distinction within man's spiritual nature, others that he is simply calling the spiritual nature by a different name, according to its associations. It is soul as connected with the body; spirit as connected with God. The Jews certainly used more than one word to describe the unseen part of man, as in the command to love God "with all the heart, and with all the soul, and with all the might" (Deut. 6 : 5). Mary began her song, "My soul doth magnify the Lord, and my spirit hath rejoiced in God my Saviour" (Luke 1 : 46), but this is probably a simple case of poetic parallelism. The author of Hebrews speaks of the word of God "piercing even to the dividing asunder of soul and spirit" (4 : 12). In view of the presence of Greek or Hellenistic influences in this epistle, it is quite likely that "soul" here means the general principle of life, and "spirit" the more sharply defined principle of rational thought. Aristotle recognized in man two souls, the "sensitive," having to do with the ordinary life-processes, and possessed also by animals; and the "rational," having to do with the life of reason, and possessed by man alone. Educated men like Paul and the author of Hebrews may have been familiar with this speculation, which would then account for their "soul and spirit" distinction. There is no reason to believe, however, that these distinctions have much *practical* significance in the New Testament, any more than "heart and soul" have in the Old Testament. In fully developed Old Testament thought, death was the disruption of body and spirit as the two sides of human life. "The dust returneth to the earth as it was, and the spirit returneth unto God who gave it" (Eccles. 12 : 7). When Jesus bade his disciples "be not afraid of them that kill the body, but are not able to kill the soul" (Matt. 10 : 28), it is plain what he means

by "soul." (Cf. Matt. 16 : 25, 26.) Yet when he died he "gave up his spirit" (Luke 23 : 46), as did Stephen a short time later (Acts 7 : 59). At the same time, it is undeniable that the New Testament speaks of a quality of spiritual life and experience for man which is "higher" than anything that is his "by nature."

All this can only mean that while both the Old and the New Testaments suggest qualitative distinctions within the spiritual side of man's nature, the general view of man is the ordinary one of body and spirit or body and soul. Both are equally the creation of God. By virtue of his soul man can hold fellowship with God. By refusing this, he puts himself in danger. This danger affects not merely his present existence, but his existence hereafter. To "save the soul" in the proper sense is, in the Scriptures, regarded as a matter of supreme importance.

The Problem of the Method of Creation. Until comparatively recent times, the entire Christian world accepted unquestioningly a certain interpretation of the origin of man. The general belief was that God had created the world out of nothing in six successive stages, each occupying a day, and that the last of these acts was the making of man's body from the dust of the earth. Having made man's body, God breathed into it the breath of life, or his own spirit, and "man became a living soul." The supposition was that the first man was created with the complete possession of all his powers. He was a perfect being as he came from the hands of his Maker, and he had no need to learn anything.

It is a fair question, indeed, whether this is the real teaching of Genesis. Under the influence of both Biblical criticism and modern science, men have reconsidered the Hebrew tradition, and have pointed out in it certain very important facts. They have shown, for example, that it is by no means the clear teaching of Genesis that God began his creative work with nothing at all—a suggestion, indeed, made by various Christian thinkers almost from the beginning—or that he completed his work in six literal days of twenty-four hours each.

Not only so, but it has been shown that the Genesis story is not self-consistent. This inconsistency is most easily explained by the supposition, which most scholars regard as a certainty, that the Genesis story is a combination of two distinct accounts of creation. We read as one what was originally two. The first account extends from 1 : 1 to 2 : 3; the second from 2 : 4 to 2 : 25. A careful study will bring to light several striking differences. The first account says nothing at all as to *how* man was made: it simply records (1) the order and process of creation; (2) God's purpose to create man; (3) the carrying out of that purpose in the production of male and female, but with no details as to the method; and (4) the designation of man as the lord of creation. In the second account, man (the male) is made *before* either plant or animal, and he is made from the dust of the ground. Having formed a man, God then makes (1) a park for the man to live in; (2) birds and animals; and (3) a woman for a helpmeet, she being formed from a rib of the man. These differences leave little doubt that there circulated among the early Hebrews, and eventually were reduced to writing, two different stories of man's origin. The traditional interpretation, however, did not recognize these differences as such. The first two chapters were treated as a unit. The *method* set forth in 2 : 7, 21, 22 was taken as explaining 1 : 26, 27, irrespective of the inconsistency of 2 : 5 and 2 : 19 with 1 : 20–25. The "days" were understood literally; the

seventh day was the day when God literally rested; and
that this was supposed to be an ordinary day is seen in
the fact that the divine resting was made the basis for
the Sabbath, or the seventh day, being treated as a
holy day or a day of rest. The possibility of the narrative being given a different interpretation in the light
of science and Biblical criticism must not permit us to
lose sight of the fact that for centuries Christian thinking for the most part treated the narrative as literal
history. It is only as we remember that that we can
appreciate the intensity of the controversy of the last
generation.

Science and Man's Origin. Modern science gives an
account of man's origin which appears to be radically
different from that of Hebrew and Christian tradition.
The right of science to investigate nature, and to "follow whither the argument leads" is unquestionable.
Science, as such, cannot be required to pay the least
attention either to the original document or to the traditional interpretation. It properly claims the right to
study the question apart from presuppositions of any
kind. It has gone directly to nature itself, on the principle that "if you put a question to nature, she will not
answer you falsely."

In pursuance of this method of direct investigation
and interrogation, science has accumulated a vast array
of evidence which leaves little doubt that the antece-
dents of man run back into remote ages. The first man
did not appear suddenly, a perfect being in complete
possession of all his powers, but he came as the climax
of a long process which involves him, at least as respects his body, in the animal creation. He has characteristics which he shares in common with other forms
of life. There is that in him which requires that he be

classified zoölogically with the higher vertebrates and mammals. There are numerous *theories* as to the relation of man's physical organization to lower forms of life. These theories may be true or false. Probably there is some truth and some falsity in all of them. But the fact of the relation, which the theory aims to account for, seems to be undeniable.

While recognizing this fact of relationship and likeness, however, we also have the right to emphasize the equally undeniable fact of difference. Man's continuity with the animal creation does not make man merely an animal. He has capacities which no animal possesses, and which put him in a category all by himself. An account of man which leaves unexplained those very qualities which make him man is clearly a defective account. It may be that an evolutionary theory can account even for these qualities—ideality, self-criticism, moral aspiration, abstract thought, and so on—but the theory will have to be a much more comprehensive and spiritual one than anything yet offered by scientific determinism. Nature makes a self-revelation in man such as we find nowhere else. Unless man is greater than the nature whence he springs, then the nature which has for offspring man the person must be in some way spiritually conceived.

Spirit Not a Function of Body. There have always been those who regard body as the cause of so-called spirit, or, more exactly, who identify feelings, thoughts, ideas, and so forth, with bodily changes. They are quite sure that the seen object is an entity, but that the mind that does the seeing and the understanding and the comparing should also be an entity—this is quite incredible! Experience is everything, it is the one thing that should be respected, but that there should be a

permanent *subject* of experience, a subject which gives
continuity to experience and preserves its meaning—
this is to believe in something to which we have no
evidence!

But this cavalier way of "bowing spirit over the
frontier" is hardly convincing. To say that self-consciousness is the function of a body which is itself unconscious is, in the words of a famous thinker, simply
to "play the fool with language." It is infinitely more
creditable to human intelligence for men to confess that
in the fact of spirit or self-consciousness they are confronted with something ultimate and therefore inexplicable, than it is for them to offer an explanation of
it that simply does not explain. There is no compulsion
on the thinker to solve all mysteries, but there is a compulsion on him to be at least honest. No psychological
theory has yet been devised which successfully explains
thought in terms of things, or spirit in terms of body.
The ordinary "common-sense" judgment that there is
an agent, a conscious self, an entity which is as real in
its way as any other entity, which, while vitally related
to the body and in many ways conditioned by it, nevertheless on occasion makes use of the body as its instrument—this judgment has not yet been overthrown.

Body Not Comparatively Insignificant. The Christian
view is that, as between the two sides of man's nature,
the primacy belongs to the spirit, but there is often
much confusion as to what this involves. To make the
spiritual superior to the physical does not mean that
the connection between the two is purely incidental. It
does not justify the ascetic custom of treating the body
with contempt, regarding it as "vile," an evil encum-
brance which is the cause of all the ills of the spirit. It
is true that the body exists for the spirit rather than the

spirit for the body, which is but to say that the body, with all its manifold relationships and activities, is to be understood through that which it makes possible. There is much to be said, therefore, for the application in this connection of the philosophical principle that "the last in execution is the first in intention." The obvious fact in the case seems to be that if there were no body there would be no spirit, hence that body is the cause of spirit. But what seems most obvious is not always most true, and the instrumental character of the body makes it at least defensible to argue that if it were not that there might be spirits, there would be no bodies. The body comes first in the Creator's *process*, but the spirit is first in the Creator's *idea*.

Nevertheless, the body is not to be regarded as a mere incident of personal existence, as though it did not much matter. So much does it matter, that without it consciousness could not come into being, and be schooled to high and holy purposes. The human body is the epitome of an ancestry inconceivably ancient, and it is also the potentiality of a self which may still continue after the body shall have dropped away. To decry instinct and impulse as "relics of the animal" is to miss the fact that instinct and impulse look forward as well as backward. They are the condition and the promise of higher life and character. To reduce all human experience to mere bodily function is false. It is just as false to make bodily function nothing. In the true Christian view, God is the God of the whole life. The processes are as much his processes as are the ends which the processes make possible. The more we understand those processes, the more we understand God.

Personality a Body-Mind Unit. Modern thought may be considered as moving in the direction just indicated. The old dualism which set body and soul over against each other in a sharp and sometimes hostile contrast is fast disappearing. The materialism which sees nothing but body and its functions is still strongly entrenched, and has the support of a popular psychology. But materialism of this sort is too superficial, too destructive of some of our deepest convictions, too ready to overlook just those sides of human experience which are most distinctive. It has a lot to say about "behavior," but it tends to leave "that which behaves" conveniently out of the account.

To get the complete idea of man as personality we need to see that there is going on a double process or a double function. There is a single reality which exists at one and the same time as "physical" and "spiritual." Each has its own law; each manifests itself in its own way; each affects the other and is conditioned by the other, and yet is different from it. An instinct, for example, involves both a physical mechanism and (in man) a conscious control. The *meaning* of the instinct is not yielded by the mechanism; it is yielded only as the instinct is related to a mind. We can define a thing only in terms of its action: what a thing *does* is a revelation of what it *is*. Personality is a power of action which is developed through a body, but which uses the body that conditions it, and manifests itself in other than bodily ways.

Not that such a view has no difficulties of its own. How about infants who die before self-consciousness emerges? How about mental defectives? How about immortality if personality is a body-mind process? We cannot hope to answer all questions. We have to say with Kant that it is the lack of knowledge that makes faith possible. The Christian faith includes both the immortality of the spirit and the resurrection of the body. We shall discuss these more fully at a later time. It must suffice to say here that immortality means the persistence beyond death of the human consciousness that first emerged here in association with a physical organization; that the resurrection of the body means that the need of the human consciousness for an instrument that makes its experience possible will be met in the future life as it is in the present; and that that "glorified body" of the future will be in some sort of *continuity* with the body of the present life without being in all respects *identical* with it. "God giveth bodies as it pleases him. There are bodies for the earthly experience, and there are bodies for the heavenly experience" (1 Cor. 15 : 46–49).

IV

MAN AS A MORAL BEING

One of the urgent problems before the Christian thinker of to-day concerns the relations of morality and evolution. For the most part, we have become accustomed to the thought that man has kinship with all other life. We have accepted the principle of continuity, whereby we think of the whole of being—at least, of created being—under the figure of a pyramid, of which the base is the inorganic, and the apex the rational and ethical. One of the unfortunate phases of the evolutionary controversy of a generation ago was the assertion, freely made by certain defenders of the evolutionary hypothesis and accepted by its opponents, that the new theory destroyed the supernatural sanctions of morality. The evolution of the moral life of man was held to be just as indisputable as that of his physical life, and just as capable of being explained by natural law. Is it possible to show that the probability that man's moral capacity and moral experience came by a long and slow process leaves the fact and the significance of morality quite untouched?

Two Preliminary Considerations. There are two preliminary considerations which should be borne in mind in any discussion of the deeper meaning of man's moral nature.

(1) With the fact of continuity there goes the emergence of differences. All things belong together, but all

things have not the same nature. The organic is based in the inorganic, yet as between the two there is a difference. In the same way, consciousness is based in the organic, yet there can be the organic without consciousness: consciousness is therefore the emergence of the new. Self-consciousness, again, in the high degree of it that characterizes man, is a late appearance in the history of life. It presupposes consciousness just as consciousness presupposes mere life: as compared with consciousness, however, self-consciousness is something new, and it is of higher worth. In other words, we are to interpret the principle of continuity in the light of the fact that there are "degrees of reality," or "orders of being," or "gradations of existence." The moral life of man may be related to the biological fact of instinct, but there is all the difference in the world between an instinctive deed and a moral deed.

(2) The nature of a fact is as it is, irrespective of our theories about it. Even although human life could be shown to have a non-human ancestry, that would not make human life other than what it is now. The supposition that a naturalistic theory of man's origin necessarily detracts from his worth is wholly false. Much more important than the question, "Whence came man?" are the questions, "What is man now? What can he do? What may he become? Whither is he bound?" It were better to interpret the beginning by the end than the end by the beginning. In any event, no explanation of the beginning can be true which does not make the end intelligible. If, for example, it is true to say of man that he is a being who ought, and who knows *that* he ought, and who can learn *what* he ought, then man still remains that kind of being irrespective of any scientific or philosophic theory of the process whereby he came to be as he is.

The Nature of Morality.   Such words as right, wrong, ought, obligation, responsibility, truth, goodness, are connected with certain capacities of human nature and certain varieties of human behavior which we have in mind when we speak of the moral. It belongs to man to be able to distinguish an ought and an ought-not, to recognize an obligation to the ought, and to experience self-approbation or self-blame, according as his attitude is one of acceptance or rejection.

Certain questions about this are easy enough to ask —as, for example, whether the "sense" or the "notion" of the ought is not a purely social product, so that a person who should grow up in entire isolation from others would be wholly without it. There is no way whatever of proving what would happen in circumstances which are themselves impossible, and it would be simply impossible for a person to grow up in such a way. And if it were proved, nothing of any particular value would have been gained. What is the value of proving something about human nature when that nature is lifted altogether outside the normal conditions of its development? What we are concerned about is not what human nature would be under conditions radically different from those that it itself prescribes, but what it is in the conditions in which we really find it. Because the moral life may be shown to be socially conditioned does not make it any less significant, for the simple reason that sociality is not something extraneous to human nature, but is one of its fundamental characteristics. Hence to say that if man were not social he would not be moral in no wise detracts from the moral, because the "if" in the case represents what is, in fact, not possible. *If* man were not social— But, then, he *is* social; he cannot but be social; his sociality is, in part, what makes him human.

Granting, then, that morality is conditioned on social contacts, we have still to consider the distinction between a given human capacity and the necessary conditions of its development. The possibilities of education in any direction are limited by the native endowments of the person being educated. The reaction to social stimulus is determined by the individual constitution. The fact that a person learns something is proof that even before he learned it the capacity for the learning belonged to him. Every conceivable consideration is against the supposition that a being not moral in original idea and intention could be made moral by a process of training administered by other beings of a like original lack. A being without such an original fundament could undoubtedly be taught to do certain things in certain ways, to obey orders, and to follow a routine; but the very essence of morality is that a person shall do or be this or that not merely in blind obedience to external commands, but because he recognizes in this or that an *ought* to which he is able to assent, but from which he is able also to dissent. Moral training as a social matter therefore presupposes that man is a teachable moral subject.

The Idea of the Better. It could probably be shown that "preference" is a characteristic of all conscious life. Preference is the recognition of one thing as more desirable than another. Birds may be supposed to exhibit this in their choice of mates, and in their selection of a nesting place. A horse will leave hay for oats, and a dog worrying a stick will drop the stick if offered a bone. Most of our so-called "animal psychology" must of necessity be very largely guess-work, since we can never ourselves occupy the animal point of view; but how else can we describe the choice of one thing as against another except as a preference? To call it instinct does not invalidate the description: if it is instinct, it is still an instinct for the better. The dog would "rather have" the bone than the stick, which again simply means that for the dog the bone is the "better" of the two.

In human life, this power of discrimination and of preference takes on an enormous range and significance. All progress depends upon it and is controlled by it. We are forever seeking, and there is just one reason for it, namely, the belief that what we seek is better than what we have. If it were not for this belief in the better, and the purpose to find it, mankind would still be in the cave. Desire is the spring of human action, and desire means on the one hand that something is desirable, and on the other hand that there is a mind judging according to degrees of desirability.

Implicit in every such judgment is a standard. We say, "This is better." But better in relation to what? Obviously in relation to some present need or purpose, or in relation to some ideal or conviction held in the mind. A judgment is in effect a measurement: one thing is put by the side of another thing and the two are compared. The thing judged may be an act or a motive or a result; the standard of judgment may be a law or an ideal or merely a personal convenience. In any case, the measuring or comparing act involves a standard. We judge that right is better than wrong, and we make that judgment irrespective of any particular situation. But this general judgment has to be particularly applied. We have to decide *what* is right, and *what* is wrong, and why? If, for example, we say "Peace is better than war," we are passing a judgment, and the standard of judgment would be, in this case, our understanding of human well-being. But there may come a time when we reverse the judgment, and say, "War is better than peace." We should not, however, have changed our standard. Human well-being would still be that by which we judged. How human well-being may best be promoted or conserved—this is the standard, and by it we determine our idea of "the better."

Conscience. Conscience is this general human power to judge as to the better, only both the standard of judgment and the field of its application are limited. The subject of a conscience-judgment is oneself, and the standard of judgment is a recognized moral right or moral wrong. Conscience therefore presupposes and involves the idea of the ought, or a sense of obligation to a law, or an ideal, or a conviction. The condition to the operation of conscience is the power to recognize that something is not that ought to be, or that something is that ought not to be.

But not *every* such recognition of discrepancy necessarily involves conscience. The discrepancy must be of a certain kind. The moral involves the right and wrong, but not all right and wrong involves the moral. The bare idea of right is much more extensive than the strictly moral. We frequently say that we ought to do this or we ought to do that, and we frequently say that something we did was right or wrong, without there being any question at all of conscience. A student engaged on a mathematical problem, for example, comes to see that his first answer is "wrong," and that he "ought" to have worked the problem in a different way. In recognizing his error, however, he feels no moral culpability, as he would if he had lied or stolen; and in working the problem as he ought, and getting the "right" answer, he may feel a certain satisfaction, but it is a satisfaction lacking the distinctly moral quality.

Within the total range of that which we believe ought

to be, there is therefore a narrower range which we characterize as the morally right or the morally desirable. This range will naturally vary with different individuals, but whatever the restriction, the correlate of this restricted range is conscience, and neither would be possible without the other. It is here that the term duty gets its meaning. Even religion depends upon this side of human nature, for a being without conscience—the power to recognize an obligation whose evasion brings or should bring self-condemnation—would be incapable of developing a religion. Conscience does its work with reference to that extent of the moral ought which we recognize as *binding upon ourselves personally*. No man can keep another man's conscience, or determine its pronouncements. When we condemn the wrong or approve the right of another, that is a moral judgment, but it is not a conscience-judgment. A conscience-judgment has to do with our own personal motives, purposes, and actions.

The Changing Standard of Judgment. We have said that man is a being who ought, who knows *that* he ought, and who can learn *what* he ought. Conscience is self-condemnation or self-approbation in view of the personal attitude to the known ought. The moral standard itself, however, according to which conscience pronounces, is not a fixed or static thing. What is approved to-day may be condemned to-morrow. If that were not so, moral progress would be impossible. To seek enlightenment is a moral obligation, and the obligation is increased as the enlightenment is increased. If one should refuse enlightenment so as to keep obligation low, one does not, after all, escape the higher obligation. The only kind of ignorance that will excuse a man before the moral law is unavoidable and unintentional ignorance. We have not grasped the majesty and the exactitude and the severity of the moral ideal until we realize that it requires us not merely to do as we believe we ought, but to employ all possible means to correct and improve the believed ought.

We are to commit ourselves to the right as God gives us to see it. But we may be self-committed to the right in principle and yet be perplexed to know the right thing to do in a given situation. There is undoubtedly an absolute right, but only God knows that. What we are held to is not this absolute right (although we shall repeatedly do the absolutely right thing), but what might be called *a working right*. This working right is our best knowable—not merely the best that we know, but the best we are able to know. Of necessity, this varies with circumstances. It differs among individuals according to their opportunities and earnestness, and it differs from time to time in the life of the same individual. We shall often disagree as to what is right: our own personal obligation is to the right as we sincerely come to apprehend it. The right in this sense will of necessity continually change. More light comes daily to the earnest soul. As experience widens, reflection leads to a change in the working standard. We are scholars in the school of life, and a scholar's business is to learn, and to adjust himself to his new knowledge.

Thus while the *form* or principle of morality is unchangeable, the *content* of it is progressive. Men may with complete conscientiousness commit themselves to what is actually wrong, supposing it to be right: there may be perfect sincerity on opposite sides of the same moral issue. This is a part of the price we pay for being growing moral creatures. But it is better that we have the possibility of error and of antagonism, and with that the possibility of moral growth, than that we should refuse to change our standards, or be unable to do so. A static morality would be mere conventionality, and it has no promise of the better. A changing morality, while the change may sometimes be for the worse, at least makes the better possible, and saves us from the deadliness of moral stagnation.

The Social Conscience.   It was said above that the field of conscience is the individual life itself, and that no man can be the keeper of the conscience of another. But one individual is always bound up with other individuals. "No man liveth unto himself." This necessary association of life with life gives rise to the possibility of collective action, and collective action cannot escape moral appraisal. The Hebrew prophets recognized this very clearly, and they called for a national repentance for national wrong-doing.

One of the encouraging features of our own day is the emphasis on group morality, with its implication of group responsibility and group self-blame. A given community will come to see that there are things connected with the community that "ought not" to exist, and there will arise a demand that they be changed. The motives for demanding the change will vary: with some men they will be simply economic, and with some even æsthetic. But other men will demand the change on purely moral grounds. The conditions, they will say, are *wrong*. The demand will be with them not a matter of economic advantage but of pure conscience.

It is proper to call this the social conscience, but it could have no existence apart from the individual conscience. There is danger of a false abstraction here. Strictly speaking, the social conscience is individual recognition of responsibility for social ill. The awakening of the social conscience is always the work of one or two far-seeing individuals, and these are the prophets of their age.

The Christian conception of the Kingdom of God is to be understood accordingly. More will be said of this later. It suffices now to say that the Kingdom of God means the carrying of the filial and fraternal spirit into all the manifold relations of life. The presupposition of this is the moral nature of man and the possibility of its indefinite education and expression. The more that men see the *inward idea* of morality, the more they will realize that its scope is universal. The progressing universalizing of the moral idea means the coming of the Kingdom of God. There are, however, difficulties here which it will require religion to overcome. God's Kingdom cannot be brought in if God himself is left out.

V

EVIL IN RELATION TO THE HUMAN RACE

We have found reasons for believing that nature and human life have their origin in the creative power of a Divine Will. We have held that the fundamental characteristics of man as a being at once rational and ethical require that similar characteristics shall be ascribed to God. Under the illumination of the Christian revelation, we have gone further even than that. Not only is God a rational and moral being, he is also such a being as is able to account for Jesus Christ. Christ is the best that we know, and God cannot be less than that: therefore there is in God not only the power and wisdom adequate to nature, but also those great moral qualities of love and tenderness and self-sacrifice of which Christ is the supreme human exponent. If this were all that needed to be said, faith would be a much simpler thing than it is.

The General Problem. The general problem is how to explain the fact that things are not so good as we believe they might be. We find in nature much that perplexes us, and the perplexity is only increased when we turn to human life. We say that a good God maintains the order of nature, and yet we see in that same order a provision for suffering, pain, and death. We say that man is in a peculiar sense the offspring of this God, made in his image, the object of his especial care; and yet this same man is often smitten by nature, he is so constituted physically that he is liable to suffering, so constituted mentally that he is liable to err, and so constituted morally that he is liable to sin.

We come, therefore, upon a deep-seated opposition. There is a discrepancy between what we would fain believe to be so and what we actually experience. Life presents us with what seems to be a vast incongruity. Men have felt the challenge of this fact from the beginning. It is not merely a speculative problem, toward the solution of which one may be more or less indifferent. It is a problem of far-reaching practical implications. No one thing has made more sceptics than this, and no one thing puts a more severe tax upon both our reason and our faith.

Evil as Relative. No discussion of this problem that seeks to go below the surface can avoid the question whether evil is absolute or relative. The terms are technical, but it is hardly possible to avoid using them. To say that evil is relative is to say that a thing is evil only by virtue of its relation to something else. To say that it is absolute is to say that evil is an essential quality of the thing judged to be evil, and that it is evil quite apart from any relations.

In this sense, there is no such thing as the absolutely evil. It may, indeed, be claimed that a completely depraved will could be so regarded—a will, that is, that had ceased either to desire or to be able to will the good. Apart from the question whether such a complete depravation is possible, it still remains that the will is judged to be evil *relatively to the good*. And this relative character is present in all evil, whatever its form. Even the fact that all living things must die cannot be regarded as an absolute evil, since death serves a great natural purpose in making possible other and perhaps better forms of life. It might be said that the necessity of death as a minister to life is an absolute evil; but even that cannot be maintained, since we can think of no good reason why individual forms of life should continue to maintain their present form indefinitely.

In a word, nothing can be shown to be evil in and of itself. Disease germs are evil only in a certain relation to living tissues, and there are conditions in which they have even a beneficent function. The same is true of all forms of poison. There is no such thing as an absolute poison: a substance is judged to be poisonous because of its effect on something else. There are animals and other forms of life that we call repulsive or dangerous—but is the baboon repulsive to its mate or the tigress dangerous to her cubs? We speak of great "natural calamities," such as cyclones, earthquakes, volcanic eruptions, drought and famine. But such things disturb us mainly because of their effect upon life, and this effect is not invariably present. That is to say, not every cyclone destroys houses, not every earthquake engulfs a city, not every volcanic eruption ruins a province. Evil therefore consists in an effect and a relation, and where there is no such effect and relation there is no positive evil.

The Standard of Judgment. It was said in the preceding chapter that every judgment involves a standard. The standard whereby we judge a thing to be evil is necessarily the good. We do not learn the good through the evil, but we learn the evil through the good. Unless we already had the idea of the good we could not judge the evil to be such. Life is a good: death is an evil because it destroys life. Sound health is a good: ill health is an evil because there is a more desirable condition. The good is therefore positive—it is that which ought to be; the evil is negative—it is that which ought not to be. The only way we can think or speak of an "ought not to be" is in relation to an "ought to be." The "ought to be," or the ideal, or the good, is therefore fundamental, primary, and positive, and it gives us the standard by which we judge anything to be evil.

This assertion that evil is relative does not mean that evil is not *real*. There is not merely the absence of the good, but there is also the presence of what is not good. Evil is not an unreality because it is a negation.

Forms of Evil. The usual classification of evil is as the natural and the moral. Natural or physical evil includes all such things as pain, material loss, hampering restrictions on the activity, the various forms of destruction, and especially death. By moral evil is ordinarily meant sin, and other forms of wrong-doing which, while not being sin in the strict religious sense, involve a responsible and blameworthy falling short of the best.

There are forms of evil which it seems impossible to include under this simple scheme. The boy who has a worthy ambition, and who through force of circumstances finds himself unable to realize it; a perplexing industrial or financial situation confronting a group of business men, for which no solution can be found; all that we mean by ugliness, or discord, or imperfection in human enterprise or achievement; the enormous amount of difficulty that comes upon men through unavoidable ignorance, their own or others; those various forms of loss and suffering and grief which befall men solely because of their social relationships—these surely are evils in some sense, yet they can hardly be called natural evils unless we give the term an unwarranted extension, and they certainly cannot be called moral evils if moral evil is sin or some other responsible fault of the will.

All this indicates how complex the problem is, and it justifies certain important distinctions being made in

the various forms of evil. Evils may be responsible or
irresponsible; they may be of the understanding or of
the will; they may be inevitable or the result of deliberate choice; they may issue in simple blame or in moral
guilt. More sharply, evil may be distinguished as inevitable and as avoidable.

Inevitable Evil. There are many people who shrink
from the conclusion that some evil is inevitable, and
yet the conclusion is apparently inescapable. Nobody
but a thorough-going determinist would say that *all*
evil was inevitable, but we may recognize the fact of
inevitable evil without being determinists. This, indeed, is in keeping with the Christian view that through
human ill the glory of God is to be manifested, and that
it is by much tribulation that we are to enter the Kingdom of God. Some would escape what they regard as
a dilemma by falling back on the familiar philosophy
that what is inevitable is not evil and what is evil is not
inevitable. But we cannot get out of a difficulty of this
sort by the simple device of constructing an epigram.
The question may be stated simply enough: "Is evil
inseparable from life?" If it is not, then it is so far
forth inevitable, but it is not thereby the less evil.
There are certain forms of evil for which the whole constitution of things makes provision. It is inevitable
that natural forces will sometimes prove destructive.
It is inevitable that forms of life will fail at times to adjust themselves rightly to their environment. It is inevitable that men will err in their judgments and fail
in their executions. It is inevitable that sorrow and
grief will come upon men because of their relations to
each other. It is inevitable even that men will on occasion do what they know to be wrong.

All this is so because God made men as they are, centres of instincts and desires and capacities, in order that they might *attain unto* a perfection, and he put them in a world suitable to this purpose. There is implied here a process of growth, of adaptation, and of use, and such a process in the case of a free being like man is attended with the certainty of continual failure. It is this certainty that justifies the term inevitable. The process involves not merely the *possibility* of evil, but the *fact* of it, and the fact not merely of natural evil but of moral evil. To state the case quite drastically, it is certain that such beings as men will not merely make mistakes, but will also commit sin in the sense of wilfully doing what is recognized as morally wrong. There is therefore attached to evil an aspect of necessity. Not that all evil is necessitated, and not that all evil is necessary. But in so far as there is evil belonging in the very nature of things, we may call that necessitated. In so far as a certain amount of evil is required to make the conditions in which souls may be grown, we may call that necessary. There is, however, always more evil than can be accounted for in this way.

Avoidable Evil.   Strictly speaking, it is only as it can be shown that some evil is avoidable and therefore unnecessary that we are justified in believing in responsibility. There is no human responsibility for the necessitated or for the necessary, and yet responsibility respecting certain evils is a quite inescapable conviction on the part of men. How can we make the feeling of responsibility rational except by connecting it with that which ought not to have been and which need not have been? Let it be granted that mistakes are inevitable: that does not mean that *every* mistake is inevitable. Let it be granted that evils inevitably come upon men by virtue of social relationships: that does not mean

that *all* of such evils are inevitable, and therefore are
without responsibility. Let the inevitableness even of
sin be granted: every particular sin is not thereby ex-
cused because not *every* particular sin is inevitable. The
certainty that men will sin does not mean that it is certain a man will fail every time he is tempted, for as a
matter of fact, temptation is repeatedly resisted in
every life. In one and another of its forms, evil will
continue to be inseparable from life: this we have to
take as a fact. But it is just as true that there is more
evil, natural and moral, than there needs to be. It is
this unnecessary and unavoidable evil that creates the
pressing practical problem. No religion is adequate
which cannot face it with courage and with confidence.

The problem naturally varies according to the nature
of the evil. The problem of the avoidable evil that
grows out of man's dependence on nature is the problem
of a better understanding and control of nature. The
problem of the avoidable evil that grows out of errors
of the understanding is the problem of truer insight and
more knowledge. The problem of the avoidable evil
that grows out of social relationships is the problem of
a more effective social control. As men increase in these
various forms of knowledge and insight and control,
certain forms of evil will grow less.

Especially is *sin* to be included among the avoidable
evils. As to that, Christianity speaks in no uncertain
tone. Sin is primarily a matter of the inward spirit and
purpose. Wherever there is a falling short of a known
or knowable good, there is a fault. But, as was said
above, not all fault comes under the category of the
moral, and only responsible and avoidable moral fault
is sin. Not every wrong thing is a sin: at some "wrong"
things we may even smile as blunders, but no one can
smile at sin. Sin is that form of wrong which consists

in the inward denial of God and his will. Sin is therefore a distinctly religious idea. Every person who is capable of forming an ideal of right and recognizing its authority is capable of sin. Guilt attaches to the rejection of this authority. Sin and guilt are inseparable, although the *consciousness of guilt* may not be present. That is to say, a sinner may be wholly indifferent with regard to his sin, but that does not make him the less guilty.

Punishment. Punishment is a form of suffering, and it is always connected with fault. Most people are convinced that much fault is never punished, and that much punishment is out of all proportion to the fault itself. There is a tendency also to confuse suffering and punishment. All punishment is suffering, but not all suffering is punishment. Indeed, one of the evils that often perplex men is just this very fact of the sufferings of the innocent and the frequent apparent escape of the guilty. Again and again we are dismayed to see what dreadful social consequences may follow from the selfishness and sin of one man. What relief there is from this is provided by the fact that the same principle of relationship that makes such consequences possible also makes it possible that one man's righteousness shall bring blessing to many others.

Punishment does not follow all fault, but in one way or another moral fault is *always* punished. The punishment may not take the form of physical or social consequences. Punishment does not have to be visible in order to be real. There is sin that is known only to the sinner himself and to God, and there is a punishment of sin that goes on unobserved by others. Sinfulness involves spiritual loss. That much of punishment is inescapable, and it obtains whether the sinner realizes it or not. More positively, there are such results as the accusations of conscience, the fear and distrust of God, the withdrawal of the divine presence, the gradual enslavement of the will, the increasing indifference to things of the spirit—and all these results are to be regarded as punishments of sin.

Punishment as Remedial and as Retributive. What has just been said would seem to justify the old distinction of punishment as remedial and as retributive. It has been customary to say that even although punishment may have a remedial purpose and result, it is nevertheless also eminently *proper*—something demanded by the very nature of the moral law itself. Even therefore when punishment fails as a corrective, it is still justifiable, and it will still continue in its retributive aspect after all hope of betterment is past. We are told, indeed, that the very fact that punishment does not cease when the guilty person remains obdurate shows that retribution is more fundamental than discipline. Permanent obduracy is surely retribution enough, and it is a retribution whose very characteristic is *hopelessness*.

Some forms of punishment are obviously remedial, in the sense that they direct attention specifically to their causes. But it is difficult to see how the moral deterioration that follows inevitably on moral evil can be anything but retributive. In what sense can increasing indifference to God be regarded as disciplinary? Sin is by no means invariably followed by the sense of guilt: it is more likely to be followed by increase of unconscious moral enslavement. This is real penalty, but if it is intended as a means of restoring the sinner, then of necessity it defeats its own purpose. If a specific moral failure is always punished by an inevitable lowering of the whole moral tone, that is a form of punishment which is in no sense remedial but is only retributive. But in that case, it is wholly without promise. It accelerates the movement of the soul away from God, whereas the turning of the soul toward God is what is wanted.

Punishment alone, therefore, can never avail to win the sinner back to God. He must be appealed to in some other way than this. There are certain organic consequences of sin which may succeed in arousing the conscience. But these consequences are variable: two different men may be punished in different ways for the same form of sin. The turning of the soul to God cannot be left to punishment, which in its outward form is uncertain, and in its inward form tends to make the return increasingly difficult. God must do more than simply punish men if he would win them.

VI

EVIL IN RELATION TO GOD

If evil is a fact of human experience, and if the will of God is the final reality with reference to which all things are to be understood, we cannot avoid asking ourselves the question how evil and God are to be related. Some will attribute evil to the influence of malign and hateful spirits. We have a form of this view in the Old Testament, for the Genesis narrative supposes that an evil power capable of tempting the first pair already existed. The idea continues into the New Testament. It is present in the Gospels (Matt. 4 : 1–10; 12 : 22–29; 25 : 41); in the Epistles (Eph. 2 : 2; 6 : 11–16; II Thess. 2 : 8, 9; II Peter 2 : 4 f.; I John 3 : 8, 10); and in the Revelation (12 : 7–17). The view only pushes the problem further back. If evil here is to be accounted for by "the devil and his angels," it is still necessary to account for these evil beings. If we are to suppose that they were created free and pure, and then voluntarily fell, that shows that evil can be accounted for without postulating other evil. In that case, we can account for moral evil in human life without falling back on demonic agency.

God Involved in Evil. In some way God is involved in evil. Many people feel a natural unwillingness to accept this conclusion: it seems to them to reflect on the divine holiness and love. It does not follow, however, that because God is in some way involved in evil **he**

must therefore be held directly responsible for it in all its forms. Some of its forms, indeed, are so obviously provided for in the very nature of things that we must suppose that God deliberately intends them. Within the scope of his will and purpose it is provided for that we shall experience difficulty, and that we shall suffer pain, and that we shall fall into error of various sorts, and that the conflict of natural forces shall issue in destruction and loss, and that suffering and sorrow shall come upon us because of our relations with each other. These things, however, are not to be regarded as ends in themselves. They are but parts of his complete will and purpose with men, potential ministers to the good that he is seeking for his children. But just because they belong in that whole which God makes possible and which he maintains, God is himself involved in them. The fact yields us one of our most perplexing problems, but it is a problem on which the Christian faith is not silent.

A consistent view will have to extend the connection of God with evil to include even sin. Not that God wants sin, and not that he directly produces it, but he maintains the conditions which make it possible, and he has a purpose which renders it inevitable. This does not preclude God from judging sin, or from punishing it, any more than a father is precluded from passing judgment on the failure of the child whom he has brought into existence. But it does mean that God shall not leave men in their sins; it does mean that he shall not pass judgment on them indifferently; and it does mean that he shall use all his resources to save the sinner and to put an end to sin.

Evil That God Does Not Prevent. We have said that there is evil that lies within the total range of the divine purpose and yet does not express the divine will. Sin is to be included in this form of evil, as is also that phase of the results of sin which consists in the suffering of the innocent. God does not will such evil, yet at the same time he does not prevent it. He does not prevent it because his purpose calls for the very conditions whence evil of this sort arises. He could prevent the evil only by changing the conditions, and he could change the conditions only by changing his purpose. With the conditions of life as they are, both sin and suffering, as we said before, are inevitable. If, however, God sets before himself a purpose which can be realized only through conditions which give rise to evil as well, his non-prevention of the evil in the interests of his purpose only the more deeply involves him in the evil.

God's Use of Evil. The evil that God does not prevent he nevertheless actively opposes and seeks to destroy. If anything can seem to justify to our minds the evil in question, it is the belief that it is an inseparable element of a purpose of good—a purpose so great that it is worth all it costs to God and man to realize it. Some shrink from the conclusion that God cannot find good except through evil: it seems to them to impeach both his wisdom and his power. Yet since this is the way that God actually is accomplishing his purpose, why may we not suppose that it is the best way? The limitations he is under pertain to the very nature of the case, namely, bringing free and finite beings to genuine moral goodness. And why should this purpose to increase the sum of goodness need any justification? We have to be the way we are or not be at all. So far as we can tell, the choice has to be between human life and experience as we actually know it, and no human life and experience at all. But conscious existence is

per se desirable. It is desirable even when it is marred
by sin and suffering. Much more is it desirable as it
approaches nearer the divine ideal.

We can best get at the question of evil in relation to
the divine purpose if we think out of the world all that
has come into it because of the way in which men have
faced their difficulties. All progress is man's purpose to
a challenge. Pain is a dreadful reality, but what sort
of human beings would be produced by a world wholly
painless? No one will deny that sin is tragic, but what
sort of creatures should we be if we were not able to
do wrong? It is because we can do wrong that we can
also do right. The ministries of love are never so great
as when the loved one is in dire need. In their island
paradise the Lotus-eaters degenerated. We may not be
able to say what kind of human beings God could produce in circumstances from which all difficulty and
hardship, all pain and suffering, all power of choice between better and worse, were absent, but it is easy to
see that they would at least *lack backbone*. Life tends
to inertia, and it needs continually to be prodded. Man
enters the kingdom through tribulation, and the same
God plans both tribulation and kingdom, and he does
that because he knows—what in our finer moments we
ourselves agree to—that the kingdom is worth all the
tribulation it costs to enter it.

God's Opposition to Evil.   An adequate understanding of the Christian religion justifies and even requires
the distinction we have been making between the evil
that God intends and does not prevent and the evil he
resolutely opposes. The man born blind, said Jesus,
was not blind as a punishment for sin. He did not pur-
sue the question further, except to add the significant
words that the blindness confronted him with an oppor-

tunity to glorify God by working a cure. But there was
nothing uncertain about Jesus' attitude when he turned
on those who objected to the cure because it was
wrought on the Sabbath. He charged them with a
blindness infinitely worse than the blindness he had
just healed. It was a blindness which, for all its pious
protestations, could not see God in the plainest way in
which God ever shows himself to men, namely, in goodness of life and in the service of love. Such blindness,
therefore, indicated a perversity of will, a confusion of
the fundamental values of life, an indifference to human
well-being in the highest sense, a total misapprehension
of God's real nature and character—and Jesus made no
secret of his opposition to it and his hatred of it. He
even declared that his own opposition and hatred were
a revelation of the opposition and hatred of God.

Evil of this kind, which consists fundamentally in a
defect at the very centre of the life, meets God's opposition because it is a violation of his law. But what
law? The law of the true fellowship of man with God
and therefore of man with man. Of necessity, such a
law is not an external thing of any kind. It is found
written in no book of statutes, and it can be enforced
by no legal penalties. There is an inward disposition
and attitude in which lies man's true good. As he finds
that, he finds the law of his life. It is a law which represents God's will for him: the law is therefore God's
law, and its violation constitutes sin. In Jesus Christ
that law, the law of man's relation to God and his fellows, is fully revealed and exemplified. To have toward
God the spirit of a son, and to have toward others the
spirit of a brother, and to see in Jesus the absolute type
of this sonship and brotherhood—this is God's purpose
with us. To be unfilial and unfraternal is to deny that
purpose, and to come into opposition with God.

Forms of God's Opposition. Apart from the question of physical suffering, God's opposition to sin takes the forms of personal loss and of social loss.

(1) Personal loss. Man is constituted for fellowship. "It is not good for him to be alone." Only in and through fellowship can he find that fulness of life in which consists salvation. He can make his own life all that it was intended to be, only as he relates it to other lives. The penalty of the self-centred life is that it becomes the victim of its own self-centredness. Not only is it making itself increasingly a stranger to the larger life, but it is also making itself increasingly unable to enter into that larger life. Selfishness carries its own penalty. The less you care about God and others, the less you are able to care. The more you want just yourself, the more you have just yourself. The narrower the range of your regard, the more restricted your real life becomes. The penalty that God attaches to sin as defined is that you become more and more satisfied with your own status. You are meant for God, but you leave him out of your life. That makes hell a *possibility*. To realize that you have lost God—and sooner or later the realization is inevitable—makes hell an *actuality*. There is no hell except as there are human souls. A soul that awakens to find itself *alone* has all the hell there is—but it is enough.

(2) Social loss. This sort of self-centredness also involves suffering and loss for others. One is appalled when one stops to consider how individual sinfulness works itself out socially and materially. Those results are as truly a revelation of God's opposition to sin, they are as truly his judgment of it as utterly bad, as are the results that fall directly upon the sinner himself. Of course, the same fact of social and physical relationship which preserves the results of our ignorance

and of our deliberate wrong-doing, preserves also the results of our righteousness, but the law in the case is God's law irrespective of the way it operates.

Evil and Divine Suffering. The Christian religion makes the far-reaching claim that among those involved in the suffering arising from evil is God himself. It makes this claim because of its view of God as a Father. The roots of the idea are already found in the Old Testament, but the supreme expression of it is in the mind of Christ. The sorrow which Jesus Christ felt in the presence of the sorrows of others, and the suffering which he endured because of sin, are but the reflection in a human life of the sorrow and suffering of God. If we want to know what the evils of the world mean to God, we have first to know what they meant to Jesus Christ. Why? Because, as he said of himself, "he that hath *understood me* hath *understood the Father.*" According to Christianity, God's point of view is always that of a Father, and a father's supreme interest is the conservation of the true life of the family for which he is responsible. The Kingdom of God is the Family of God, and what a father wants is not subjects but sons. But when the sons rebel, when they are disloyal to the spirit and purpose of the Family, what shall the Father do? He must deal with them "as with sons," but this will not preclude the use of severe methods. Indeed, it is just because of the Fatherhood that the severity will be adopted. If God dealt with sin "softly," he would fail to make us see what sin really is. The severity is not for its own sake, but for the sake of the relationship which the Father seeks with his children. All the evil that comes upon men is embraced in the total purpose of God the Father, whether that evil be disciplinary, educative, penal, or vicarious. But just because God is a Father, the sufferings of the children are his sufferings, also. When men will not bear themselves toward him as they *should*, he is unable to bear himself toward them as he *would*. He is grieved when men sin, and severely though he may deal with them, even to the point of being "angry" and "wrathful," the grief persists throughout the severity, and may, indeed, be increased by that very severity.

All this, of course, is to speak of God under a very definitely human point of view. It is none the less the Christian way, and to eliminate it in the interest of a philosophical theory that points out the difficulty in the idea of a suffering God, is to lose everything and gain nothing. There is value in the idea that God suffers. There is no value in the idea that he does not. At this point, if nowhere else, we are justified in insisting that the value of the idea, and the results of denying it, are evidence to its reality.

Redemptive Suffering. We find that in human life, suffering for others may be a great redemptive force. It is redemptive not only as a spectacle—as when a boy breaks down at the sight of the sorrow his sin has brought upon his mother—but as a motive leading to the adoption of every possible effort to win back the wanderer. We saw before that the worst form of penalty, deterioration of character, and the increasing tendency toward the self-centred life, was hopeless: it contains in itself no promise of betterment. God could therefore never win men to himself merely by punishing them, or by so devising life that suffering is inseparable from error. He suffers in the penalties that he lays upon them, but such suffering does not *satisfy* him because the penalties in question are not restorative. The consequences that follow on the filial and fraternal relation being ignored will show how fundamental the relation is, but they do not in themselves contain any promise of its being realized. Indifference to God's will simply produces the attitude of a still deeper indifference.

God can bring men to the relation that he seeks for them only as he can break down this indifference, and purely penal means can never do this. Penalty may make men prudent as to the *kind* of wrong-doing in which they indulge, but it cannot destroy the *inward spirit* which is the root of the wrong-doing. It is from the standpoint of this fact that we are to understand Jesus Christ. In him God made final and complete exhibition of his fatherly nature and will. The divine heart has been laid bare, and in such a way as to show at one and the same time what sin means, what God will do to destroy it, and what that is in which man's good truly lies.

VII

THE JESUS OF THE FIRST THREE GOSPELS

We can never properly understand Jesus Christ unless we see him first of all as a historical character. He was an actual human being. He appeared at a definite time in the world's history. He entered into the life of his nation. He engaged in the usual human occupations. A few men who knew him personally put his life on record. No interpretation of him can pretend to be valid which does not treat this record fairly.

The Written Sources. Our knowledge of the life of Jesus is confined very largely to the Gospels of Matthew, Mark, and Luke. These are called "The Synoptic Gospels," because we have to "see them together" to get a complete view of Jesus. The Fourth Gospel supplements the story at various points, as, for example, the *length* of the public ministry, which in the Fourth Gospel extends over three Passovers, whereas the Synoptic Gospels mention only one Passover and seem to limit the ministry to a single year. The Fourth Gospel, however, was written in the closing years of the first century, and contains too large an element of theological interpretation to make it strictly historical. The other writings of the New Testament help to confirm the Gospel story, but they add practically nothing to our knowledge of the historical Jesus.

The Synoptic Gospels present many critical problems which do not concern us here. It must suffice to say that scholars incline to date their appearance in their present form somewhere between 60 and 70 A. D. There are, however, various strata in the Gospels as we now know them, and these strata cover much of the preceding twenty or thirty years. It is very clear that Mark is the earliest of the three, and there is a sound tradition that Mark was the spokesman for Peter. Most of Mark was incorporated into Matthew and Luke, but these two Gospels also contain material peculiar to each, and material common to both but not found in Mark. For example, peculiar to Luke are certain details of the Infancy and the parable of the Prodigal Son; peculiar to Matthew are the bulk of the "eschatological" discourses in chapters 24 and 25; and common to Matthew and Luke but not found in Mark are many of the "sayings" of Jesus, collected by Matthew into "The Sermon on the Mount," but more often placed by Luke in their historical setting.

Briefly, documents dealing with our Lord began to appear soon after his death, and these, together with oral traditions and the testimony of eye-witnesses, were freely employed by the compilers of our Synoptic Gospels. The result is a description of the life of Jesus which is so nearly contemporary that it can be accepted as essentially trustworthy.

The Son of Man. There was never any doubt as to the genuine humanness of Jesus in the minds of those who knew him best. Apart from the incident in the Temple in his twelfth year, we can only guess at what went on in his life during "the silent years" at Nazareth. It is incredible, however, that his experience at his baptism should have come without preliminary preparation. Already John had begun a ministry of baptism unto repentance in Judæa. Jesus came from Galilee to Judæa, perhaps to a feast at Jerusalem, but more likely to associate himself with the work of his kinsman John. He insisted on being baptized, and the conclusion is irresistible that he felt in himself some deep moral and spiritual need which he hoped the baptism would be a means of satisfying.

We can understand the ensuing temptation only in the light of what happened at the baptism. A growing conviction now became intensified, and it became necessary for him to face the implications of this conviction. He was the Father's "well-beloved Son," but what does that mean, and what does it require him to do? That is the subject of the long struggle in the wilderness. It was the struggle of a man seeking to know what he must do with his life—whether to attract attention in some spectacular way, or whether to give himself wholly into the hands of God, and follow each day the path that each day presented. The fasting, the dialoguing, the different forms in which the temptation is presented, the ministration of angels—these are all incidental. What is central is the depiction of a human soul, conscious of a divine call, eager to obey the call, but uncertain as to all that the call involves, and waiting upon God to dispel the darkness.

The entire ministry of Jesus should be looked at in the light of this experience. He was temptable: therefore he was human. The clue to the understanding of the Gospel Portrait is found not in the dreams of Joseph as to the Babe, and not in the visions of the gentle Mary, but in this fact—that Jesus never wavered in his determination to submit himself wholly to the will of God, while yet he was not always certain as to what that will for himself might be.

A Religious Experience. The Jesus presented in the Gospels is a profoundly religious man. Religion is in the communion of man with God, and the more sustained the communion the more the human takes on the quality of the divine. Outside of the infancy narratives, all the Gospels introduce us to Jesus at a moment when he is overwhelmingly conscious of the presence and favor of God. This consciousness continued with him to the end. There are times, as in the case of the Transfiguration, when others were present with him as he prayed. There are other times when he retired into solitude to commune alone with God. Indeed, it is a striking fact that the Synoptic Gospels, while they continually refer to Jesus' habit of praying, nowhere report any of his prayers, if we except "The Lord's Prayer," and one or two brief petitions.

The evidence to the religious faith of Jesus is not in the fact that men saw him often at his devotions, but in the whole attitude of his life, in his moral poise, in his unsullied purity, in his absolute confidence that he is under divine leadership, in his utter devotion to the Kingdom of God, and in his ready acceptance of everything that awaited him in the fulfillment of his vocation. Nobody could have appeared before men as Jesus did, or could have borne himself to men as Jesus did, who did not know "the secret place of the Most High."

Jesus' Belief about Himself. In considering this question, it is necessary for us to free our minds as much as possible from later statements about Christ in the various historical creeds. What we desire is to get a fresh first-hand impression of him as he appeared to others and as he believed himself to be.

Jesus believed that he had direct connection with God's purpose to save men. His thought as to what this involved underwent considerable change. As we saw before, he is perplexed at first as to the sense in which he is "Son of God," and there are those who question whether during his lifetime he ever thought of his sonship in any other terms than that of a peculiarly intimate moral relation. There is certainly a growing sense of confidence in the Divine Father, and after the confession of Peter at Cæsarea Philippi and the Transfiguration a growing sense that his entire commitment of himself into the Father's hands will take him by a way that ends in death.

Speaking quite generally, we may say that the early part of Jesus' ministry is characterized by the good works and the gracious words anticipated by his opening pronouncement in the synagogue at Nazareth; and that the latter part is characterized by a gradual concentration upon the needs of his more intimate disciples, an increasing note of severity in his dealing with those who spurn his tidings of good, and a conviction that only by a tragic death at Jerusalem can he say and do all that God sent him to say and do.

A Doer of His Own Word. This indicates that Jesus' message was in very much more than a spoken word. Those who heard him declared that never man spake as he did. He taught men the truth about themselves. He showed them the depths of their own heart, and where the roots of sin lay. He enunciated principles—all of them reducible in the end to love to God and love to men—which contain in themselves the promise of the universal Kingdom of God. But he did more than speak. He *acted*. The truth he uttered was incarnated in his own life. What he called others to be, that he was himself.

Jesus declared to men that they could be saved only as God the Father had absolute right of way in their lives. In "setting his face to go toward Jerusalem" he was revealing his willingness to face the logic of his own declaration. He came to establish the Kingdom of God, but he could not establish it with words. The Kingdom of God is finally not principles but lives, not maxims but characters. Jesus established the Kingdom by completely embodying its principles and its maxims. To learn what the Kingdom is and means we must look at him. There was nothing he said about God the issue of which he did not himself face.

The Miracle of Himself. Not only was Jesus greater than his own message; he was greater than his own great deeds. The record makes it plain that he did things which created a profound impression upon the observers. His followers said he had a power from God; his enemies said his power was from the Evil One. As a matter of fact, the miracles occupy a far smaller place in the record than is usually supposed, and many of them are "cures" which it is possible to account for on natural grounds. The movement he initiated did not begin in miracle at all, for he had already formed the nucleus of the Kingdom before he did any mighty work. It is not the spoken word of Jesus, and it is not his unusual deeds, that convey most powerfully his message to men. *Rather is it the man himself.* Behind the word is the Speaker; behind the deed is the Doer. It is that vital personality that we want to reach, and the words and deeds have value chiefly as they help us to find him. Jesus is greater than his greatest deeds, and he would have been no less great had he left these deeds undone. If therefore we must call the deeds miracles, much more must we call Jesus himself a miracle.

His Final Testimony in Death. To say that Jesus died as a victim of mob injustice is to leave wholly out of the account the man himself. The circumstances leading up to his death were purely incidental. Perhaps not at the beginning, but many months before the end he saw that *his death was implicit in his mission*. Had he sought to evade death, he would have left his message incomplete. He was not merely caught in a net of outward circumstances. Instead, he was the subject of a great personal conviction that he must suffer and die for men in order to complete his work. He was to bring salvation to men, and he was to do it by so wholly giving himself up to God that henceforth God would have an instrument through which, sooner or later, he could reach every single human life. The death which seemed to everybody to be the end of both himself and his work is precisely the point of his triumph. It was there and then that he supremely revealed his sonship and brotherhood. His sonship was perfected in the very fact that it maintained itself in circumstances which seemed flatly to deny God's fatherly regard. His brotherhood was perfected in the same way. To trust when one is forsaken, to love when one is hated—this is the supreme achievement of the human spirit, and Christianity was born of that achievement of the spirit of Jesus.

A Man of His Time. Jesus was a member of the Jewish race. The usual Jewish customs were observed in connection with his infancy and boyhood. He attended the national feasts. He went regularly to the synagogue. He paid taxes. His illustrations are from the life and customs of the time. His mind is steeped in the religious literature of his people. His personal habits are those which are common to the period. He mingles freely with all sorts and conditions of men. For a while it seemed as though his outlook would be entirely national, and it is only slowly that the national outlook is replaced by the universal.

In one particular respect his ideas have a local color. Believing himself to be the expected Founder of the Kingdom of God, he associates with himself many of the current beliefs about this Kingdom and him who should bring it. This explains those elements of his teaching which have to do with his "second advent" to the accompaniment of resurrection, upheaval, and wide-spread tribulation. Such views about the Messiah and his Kingdom were popular at the time, and he uses them as an instrument for expressing his consciousness of his own relation to the expected Kingdom.

A Man of No Time. Nevertheless, Jesus is really timeless. We must understand him by means of his historical setting, but what we thus come to understand we see to be of universal availability. Christianity is a product of Palestine, but it can be made at home anywhere. Jesus made no requirements as to sex, race, or social position; he specified no particular external ways of acting; with the exception of the Lord's Supper and, perhaps, baptism, he laid down no religious forms. Christianity is neither Occidental nor Oriental, but universal.

All this can be said because Jesus' supreme concern was with *man as man*. For him every man was a child of God and a brother of his kind—if not actually, at least ideally. If he could get men to look up to God and say "My Father," and if he could get men to look into each other's face and say "My brother," and if he could get men to carry out in themselves all that it *means* to call God Father, and all that it *means* to call men brother—if he could do that, he would make out of every man what God intended every man should be.

This is salvation, as Jesus understood it, and there is no other.

What is the principle of its realization? So far as Jesus is concerned, just one thing—*love*. He did not use the word in any sentimental sense. Faith, unselfishness, the pure heart, service, singlehearted devotion to the good of another—all this is in Jesus' idea of love. In such a love, a lower self is lost, but a higher self is found. Jesus was himself the supreme exponent of this spirit of sacrificial love. The salvation he proclaimed is open to all on the same conditions. A given man's salvation is in the degree in which he has Christian love. The more of such love there is in the world, the more the Family of God approaches its realization.

The Element of Mystery. There may be those who will question if this attempt to portray the Jesus of the Gospels has made enough of his birth, his miracles, and his resurrection. They will want more mystery. But is not the real mystery of Jesus less in such facts as these than in the fact that he is the creator of a universal salvation? He has brought to men the thing that men supremely need, and there is no way of accounting for him except his own way, namely, as one "sent from God" for this very purpose. He is too big to be accounted for by anything that went before him, or by anything around him. In his significance for human life on its religious side, he stands absolutely alone. That is the mystery of Jesus, and nothing can ever destroy it or make it any less.

This position enables us to meet those who suppose that the sole claim to Christ's divinity lies in such things as his virgin birth, his miracles, and his resurrection. We can remain undisturbed when we are told that the birth-story in Matthew is not convincing, and that it is by no means clear that Luke intends to deny human paternity to Jesus. We can, if necessary, agree that there may be exaggeration in the account of some of the miracles. Criticism of this sort, however, can in no wise destroy the miracle of the spiritual power which has never ceased to flow from him to men. So, too, of the resurrection narratives. Let those who wish to do so declare that it is for them incredible that a dead body was restored to life, and thereafter "went up" into heaven. Nevertheless, the evidence is irresistible that the disciples *came to a conscious experience of the presence of their Lord after they had seen him crucified and buried*. The experience utterly changed their outlook. It destroyed their dejection. It surcharged them with a zeal and a devotion that stopped at nothing. Men who had sometimes been hesitant when their Master was with them in the flesh, ceased to be hesitant after they had met him in the spirit.

One man finds evidence to Christ's divinity in his birth of a virgin, in his miracles, and in his resurrection, understood as a return to bodily life. Another finds it in the new life and power which through him have come into the world. In either case, we meet a Christ who can properly be described only as "supernatural." The supposition that Christ can be robbed of all unusual significance by the simple device of denying that he was virgin-born, or that he wrought miracles, or that he arose from the dead, is not well-founded. His meaning for the spiritual life of men as a fact of present experience would still remain, and this is made the more mysterious and the more inexplicable if the miraculous features of the record are denied. That one who was in himself a divine being should do for men all that Christ has done is what we should expect in the nature of the case. To deny that he was divine, therefore, does not lessen the mystery of his person and his power: if anything, it only deepens it, for one who is held to be "in all respects like as we are" has nevertheless done for mankind what none other has ever done. He has brought man and God together. Is not that undeniable fact best accounted for by the belief that he in some way partakes of the nature of each?

VIII

JESUS IN THE EARLY CHRISTIAN CENTURIES

Many people confess to perplexity when they turn from the presentation of Jesus in the Synoptic Gospels to the presentation of him in early Christian theology. They are impressed with what seem to them to be radical differences in the two views. Biography has given way to speculation, history to interpretation, fact to theory. That this is the case must be frankly recognized, and it creates a pressing modern problem, namely, the extent to which the early Christian speculation about Jesus yielded results which are still valid and authoritative.

The Right of Interpretation. The interpretation to which Jesus was subjected by early Christian thought sprang from a quite inevitable impulse. Any religion tends to become intellectualized. There could not be a religious experience unless there were some kind of religious belief to begin with, and the experience not only claims to justify the belief, but it also gives rise to still other beliefs. The attempt to show the relation between experience and belief gives rise to a theology. A scientific theology is therefore a friend of religion. A Christian theology quickly appeared, and was an attempt to justify the Christian religion from the standpoint of reason.

Strictly speaking, we should distinguish between the New Testament interpretation of Christ and the interpretation of the second to the fifth centuries. The factors in the interpretation were, however, the same in each case, namely, (1) History, (2) Experience, (3) The Interpreter's World-View, and (4) The Guidance of the Spirit.

History and the Interpretation. The history in question is comprised of such facts as the life and character, the work and teaching, the death and resurrection of Jesus Christ. The presupposition of the New Testament epistles—the first Christian theologies—is that incomparable personality which is the theme of the first three Gospels. It is, indeed, possible to compose a brief biography of Jesus from these epistles. Sometimes the interpretation is based on first-hand observation: "That which we have seen and heard declare we unto you" (I John 1:3). Sometimes it is based upon instruction received from personal eye-witnesses, as in the case of Paul: "I delivered unto you first of all that which also I received" (I Cor. 15:3). Sometimes there is doubt as to the source of the writer's knowledge, as, for example, the man who wrote: "God hath at the end of these days spoken unto us in a Son" (Heb. 1:2). But in every case there is *a real history* implied, the history of the actual person, Jesus.

Experience and the Interpretation. The New Testament interpreters had had an experience, and they had seen a like experience come to others. Peter could say to the men of Jerusalem: "Him whom ye slew did God exalt with his right hand to be a Prince and a Saviour, to give repentance to Israel, and remission of sins" (Acts 5:31). Paul could write to the Christians at Rome: "Being therefore justified by faith, we have peace with God through our Lord Jesus Christ" (Romans 5:1). The unknown author of Hebrews could write: "He is able to save to the uttermost them that draw

near unto God through him, seeing he ever liveth to
make intercession for them" (7 : 25). And in the Revelation we read of "Jesus Christ, the faithful witness,
the first-born of the dead, the ruler of the kings of the
earth, who loveth us, and loosed us from our sins by
his blood, and made us to be a kingdom, to be priests
unto his God and Father" (1 : 5, 6). What all these
different men say in effect is that through Jesus Christ
they and others have come to the experience of peace
with God in the forgiveness of their sins, and that he
who makes this possible is in very truth Saviour, Redeemer, Lord, Mediator, Son of God, "of whom and
for whom are all things."

The Interpreter's World-View. All the later writers
of the New Testament are concerned with the same
facts and the same experiences, yet the form of statement differs considerably. The reason for that difference is largely in the differences of mental background
and point of view of the various writers.

The earliest Christian preaching is that of Peter in
the opening chapters of the Acts. The point of view is
distinctly Jewish. Peter labors to show that Jesus is
the fulfillment of "the promise" of a new outpouring of
the Holy Spirit, and of the coming of a second David.
The Epistle of James manifests the spirit of the Hebrew
prophet. Its emphasis is on righteous conduct, and
Jesus is called Lord in the sense of his being the source
of moral authority in the Christian community. The
Epistle to the Hebrews is written against the background of the Alexandrian philosophy, which sought to
combine the spirit of Plato with the spirit of Judaism.
Plato taught that "things" are the "copies" of eternal "ideas." The author of Hebrews applies this to
the entire Jewish sacrificial system, which he conceives

as consummating in Christ, who was at once High
Priest and Sacrifice because he offered himself. The religious service inaugurated by Moses was "a copy and
shadow of the heavenly things" (8 : 5), but it was "not
the very image of the things" (10 : 1). All that is here
anticipated and symbolized finds its real "substance"
in Christ: "He taketh away the first that he may
establish the second" (10 : 9). The Fourth Gospel,
the latest important writing of the New Testament, is
written from a similar standpoint, only without the
emphasis on Jewish sacrifice. The author's philosophy
is that there is in God, as a part of his very nature, an
eternal principle of life and light. With the Alexandri-
ans, he calls this the Logos, or the Eternal Word. This
Logos "became flesh and dwelt among us" as Jesus
Christ. He brings to men what God had purposed from
the beginning. Jesus is therefore "the life and the light
of men," and as such is divine.

The most versatile interpreter in the New Testament
is Paul. He verily becomes all things to all men, that he
might win some. In Romans he presupposes that view
of the world and of human history which characterized
the Rabbinical Judaism in which he had been trained.
But while he presupposes it, he also shows that it necessarily requires far more than it was able to supply.
He interprets Christ accordingly—as the Second Adam,
as the Head of a New Humanity, as the Bearer of the
Divine Grace. The Law reveals what God demands,
but man, through his sinful nature inherited from
Adam, cannot meet it, and therefore stands condemned
and lost. In Christ, God provides a new way of salvation, the way of faith (5 : 8, 19, 21). This thought of
Christ as Saviour because he delivers from "bondage"
is also characteristic of Paul's argument in Galatians
(4 : 3–5). In Ephesians, however, there is a suggestion

of the Greek or Alexandrian point of view. Human history is thought of as the manifestation in time of an "eternal purpose" (3 : 11), the character of which remained a "mystery hid in God" (3 : 9) until Christ came. In Christ is made known to us "the mystery of God's will" (1 : 9), which is "to sum up all things in Christ" (1 : 10). Christ is therefore the instrument of God's eternal purpose to secure a "household" (2 : 19), "a holy temple" (2 : 22), a "church" (1 : 22). Something of the same point of view is revealed in Colossians, except that Paul dwells more fully upon the "pre-eminence" of Christ (1 : 18). He does this because the Colossians were in danger from a gnostic philosophy which dealt much in "thrones, dominions, principalities, and powers." Over these Paul says that Christ triumphed "openly" (2 : 15). Wherefore "he is of higher rank than all things, and in him all things hold together" (1 : 16, 17). Christ is that Central Figure through which are to be understood all God's relations with his universe.

The Guidance of the Spirit. The early Christian thinkers believed that their attempt to interpret Christ and the experience that came through him was under divine control. Paul says that he spoke the truth in Christ, and had the witness thereunto of the Holy Spirit (Romans 9 : 1); and again he says that the things he had come to know about the mystery of the crucified "Lord of Glory" had been revealed to him "through the Spirit" (I Cor. 2 : 10). The Seer of Patmos makes a similar declaration (Rev. 1 : 10, 11). This is in keeping with the promise of Jesus to his disciples, that there should come to them "the Spirit" to guide them into a fuller understanding of the truth (John 15 : 26, 27; 16 : 12, 13). We are not to suppose that the authority of the interpretation extends to the *form* in which it was cast. The guidance of the Spirit was to assure the *truthful and persuasive presentation of Christ*, but it does not necessarily validate Paul's Rabbinical theories or the Alexandrianism of Hebrews and the Fourth Gospel. Christ's power to save men does not depend upon the correctness of Paul's theory about the sin of Adam.

The Course of Later Speculation.   The New Testament interpretations of the Christian history and experiences gave rise to the problem of the following centuries.   Christ was confessed as a being who was at one and the same time human and divine, Son of Man and Son of God.   The problem was, How could he be that?

The men known as *The Apostolic Fathers*, such as Clement of Rome, Barnabas, Hermas, Ignatius, and Polycarp, were for the most part satisfied to say simply that Jesus was the incarnation of a heavenly, spiritual, divine being, the Son of God born of a virgin, and by virtue of his death the Redeemer of the world.   Their successors, the so-called *Apologists*, had to grapple with the problem in a large way, for it was their chief concern to make Christianity appear reasonable to the men of their time.   On the whole, they followed the Logos-idea of the prologue of the Fourth Gospel, only they were not agreed as to whether the pre-existent Logos (Word) was "He" or "It"—a person or a principle.   Tertullian, for example, could say: "There was a time when the Father had no Son."   Irenæus, on the other hand, held that the Logos who became incarnate in Jesus Christ always had been personally distinct from the Father, and yet had always shared in the Father's glory and power.   This was the thought elaborated by *The Alexandrian Theologians*, Clement and Origen.   With the idea of the eternal begetting of the

Son, however, Origen associated the idea of his eternal subordination.

Inevitably, these speculations met with protest, chiefly on the ground that they endangered the unity or oneness of God. The protesters are generally called *Monarchians*. Some of them protected the divine unity by making God the incarnate Son and God the Father one and the same being; others did it by making Christ a temporal manifestation of one mode or aspect of the being of God; and yet others did it by regarding Jesus as a purely human being who advanced step by step until he attained a supernatural rank.

Out of this situation there arose the great controversy between the *Arians* and the *Athanasians*. Athanasius represented those who would be satisfied with nothing less than a Christ who was divine in the most absolute sense. Arius represented those who were protesting against what seemed to them a species of polytheism. The struggle came to a head at the Council of Nicæa, in 325 A. D. This council finally adopted a creed in which it was declared that Jesus Christ was "the only-begotten of the Father, of the being of the Father, God of God, Light of Light, very God of very God, begotten, not made, of one substance with the Father." In 381, at Constantinople, another council reaffirmed and elaborated this Nicene Creed, and again declared it to represent the true Christian faith.

The controversy, however, still continued, and the Council of Chalcedon, in 451, set forth with still greater emphasis what had more and more come to be regarded as the orthodox view. This council was concerned with *the constituents of Christ's person, and the way in which they were related.* Three different views had been advanced in the church. One was that of *Apollinaris,* who found in man three elements—body, soul, and spirit. He held that the body and soul of Jesus were purely human, but that the place of the spirit—the seat of rationality and self-determination—was taken by the divine Logos or Word. A second view was that of *Nestorius*, which was to the effect that the man Jesus was a complete man—body, soul, and spirit— and that his union with the Logos was not a union of nature, nor of substance, but of will—a moral and spiritual union. A third view was that of *Eutyches*, who held that in the Incarnation the divine so over- whelmed the human that there was virtually in Christ only one nature, the divine. This was a denial of the view, ably expressed by Cyril of Alexandria, and al- ready deeply enshrined in Christian thought, that one and the same personal subject possessed equally all human qualities and all divine qualities. A human nature and a divine nature so united as to make "the one Christ."

With these various views in mind, the bishops of Chalcedon affirmed of Christ that he was "perfect in Godhead and also perfect in manhood; truly God and truly man, of a rational soul and body; consubstantial with the Father according to the Godhead, and consub- stantial with us according to the manhood, . . . to be acknowledged in two natures, inconfusedly, unchange- ably, indivisibly, inseparably." The presence in Christ of the "rational soul" is affirmed against Apollinaris' view that the human spirit was replaced by the Logos. The presence of two natures, without division and with- out separation, is affirmed against Nestorius' view that there was merely a moral union between the human Jesus and the divine Logos. The affirmation that the two natures co-existed without confusion and without mutation is aimed against the view of Eutyches that in the Incarnation the human was wholly lost in the divine.

writings, however, he is Lord because he is Saviour, and the Lordship assigned to him has a unique quality because of the character of the salvation. He is Lord as no other is Lord because he is Saviour as no other is Saviour. He saved men because he gave himself to the uttermost: he has therefore the right to ask those whom he saves to surrender themselves as utterly to his purposes.

"A Saviour, who is Christ the Lord." Thus was the birth of Jesus heralded. The New Testament is concerned to show that a history and an experience confirmed the announcement. The thinkers of the early Christian centuries are concerned with the same history and the same experience. Their theologies may cease to satisfy us, and we may seek a new one. But the test of a Christian theology will still be in the extent to which it preserves the two fundamentals: Christ the Saviour, Christ the Lord.

JESUS IN THE TWENTIETH CENTURY

It was said in the last chapter that there are many signs that the formula of Chalcedon concerning the person of Christ is failing to satisfy the modern mind. Yet the strength of this traditional view is still very great, and there are untold numbers of earnest Christian people who believe it is final. It is enshrined in the ritual of the church, in its hymnology, and in all its numerous confessions. It is wrought into the childhood memories of most Christians, and it is so much a part of the language of devotion that even those who are convinced that the view is outgrown still continue to use the language in which it has been expressed. The problem of the twentieth century will be how to relate the Christ of the Creed of Chalcedon with the rediscovered Jesus of the Gospels.

The Desire for a New Interpretation. The desire for a new interpretation does not spring from wilful destructiveness. It is found in men who are deeply interested in all that has come to be associated with the name of Christ. They are concerned for the church. They are utterly committed to Christ as their Saviour and Lord. They believe as intensely as any man believed that in Christ alone is there any hope of the world's salvation. They want to see his spirit prevail in all human life—individual and social, political and economic. But they believe that the traditional view concerning his person and work, useful though it has been in the past, is becoming a handicap. They claim that the view is the outgrowth of a philosophy which is rapidly being displaced. They believe it is possible to express all the moral and spiritual significance of Christ under a form that takes account of the modern view of things. They believe that only thus is it possible to close up the widening gap between the modern mind and Christianity. Such ideas as those of evolution, divine immanence, and personality as an organ of nature, have come to stay, and Christian theology must take account of them.

Criticism and the Traditional View. The weakening of the traditional view is largely the result of criticism, applied to (1) The Gospel Record; (2) The Creedal History; and (3) The Creedal Formulæ.

(1) Criticism and the Gospel Record. Modern criticism has in general assumed that the Gospels are to be treated like any other historical documents. It refuses to allow any theory of inspiration to preclude the right of reason and scholarship to make such an investigation. It supposes that the same vicissitudes that attended the production and preservation of other ancient documents attended these. It sets before itself as its aim the discovery of the actual Jesus through the various representations that men made of him. The critics remind us that there are differing accounts of the same event; that the records contain palpable inconsistencies, that we owe the accounts of Jesus to men who accepted the credulities of their time, and who were strongly prejudiced in favor of a supernatural view of his person; and they claim that all this must be allowed for as we try to discover the Jesus of history.

Attention is also called to the different ways in which Christ is set forth in the later writings of the New Testament. These different ways we have already

considered. The point of view of the writer, and the
purpose he had in mind, were factors determining the
form of presentation. Have we, for example, the same
explanation of Jesus in Acts 2:36 and Philippians
2:5–11; in John 20:31 and Hebrews 1:1–4? If not,
which explanation is the "final" one?

(2) Criticism and the Creedal History. In our own
day an attempt has been made to see the early creeds
in relation to their immediate circumstances. Candor
compels the statement that some of these circumstances were little short of disgraceful. Scenes of vio-
lence were far from uncommon in connection with early
church councils. Political influence was sometimes exerted. Representation was not always fair to the contending parties. Inevitably the decisions reached were
more or less the result of compromise, since it was
necessary to reconcile, as far as possible, different
points of view.

The necessity of what was done must, of course, not
be lost sight of. For the most part, the men who engaged in the framing of these definitions and statements
concerning Christ were deeply concerned for the Christian cause. They would take the world captive for
their Lord, and they would so present him as to justify
the claim. They believed that he had come to save the
world, and that he could not do this unless he were
different from every one else. It was their purpose so
to set him forth that the uniqueness of his person and
the saving power of what he did should be at once protected and explained.

Obviously, however, this was a procedure involving
a measure of speculation. Those who engaged in it
used of necessity the philosophical terms that were
common to the time. The bases of the philosophy were
largely Greek—more exactly, Hellenistic—and upon

them men sought to superimpose the Christian facts. They did that for two main reasons: because they wanted an adequate intellectual comprehension of their own faith, and because they wanted to show to others that Christianity was not merely one more religion, but that it was also the crown of all that search for truth and salvation in which men had always been engaged. Not only had the thinkers of that period a *right* to do this: they were under a certain *obligation* to do it in the interests of their cause. The modern thinker claims the same right, and believes he is under the same obligation.

(3) Criticism and the Creedal Formulæ. According to the most common traditional view, prior to the Incarnation Jesus had a divine nature; by means of the Incarnation he took on a human nature; and after the Ascension he still retained the two natures. During his lifetime, therefore, he was "two natures in one person," very God and very Man, and he remains that forever.

An increasing number of men feel that this is not a fair account of the Jesus of the Gospels; that it requires a forced interpretation of his self-consciousness as the world's Saviour; that it calls for a view of God that is in effect polytheistic; and that it gives us a person who, so far from being both God and man, is neither one nor the other.

Certainly the underlying philosophy is open to criticism. The formula, "two natures in one person," presupposes a difference between "nature" and "person." But there is no such thing as a divine nature apart from a divine person, or a human nature apart from a human person. We have the nature only as we have the person. "Two natures" therefore calls for two persons, whereas Jesus Christ was one and the same unitary person throughout all his earthly life.

Much the same criticism is to be offered of the formula, based on Philippians 2 : 5–8, that an eternal divine being became man by an act of "self-emptying." He laid aside the prerogatives of deity, and entered into our human lot. He is the same being, but his experience is different. But in what proper sense can one say that the little child who lay in Mary's arms was identical with the Creator of the worlds? In what proper sense was one who prayed to God identical with the God to whom he prayed? In what proper sense was one who at the beginning of his public career did not know how his career would eventuate, identical with a being whose right it was to know all things, past, present, and future?

Motives of the Modern View. The modern view of Jesus, in distinction from the traditional view, results from a twofold determination, namely, the determination, on the one hand, to retain him in the place of moral and spiritual supremacy, and the determination, on the other hand, to set forth this supremacy in keeping with all the facts that investigation has brought to light. The value of the ancient formulæ for those who drafted them and for those who have been able to accept them is not questioned. But at the same time the contention is made that if the ancient formulæ are losing their hold, then it is in the interest of Christianity itself that it be seen that Christ is bigger than any formula, and that old formulæ may disappear and new ones take their place while yet the Christ of the history and of the experience remains unchanged, the same yesterday, to-day, and forever.

The following discussion emphasizes those aspects of the life and work of Jesus which are more and more likely to prevail in the thought of men.

Jesus a Real Human Being. Jesus Christ was in some peculiar sense connected with God and his purpose in the world. On that the voice of history speaks clear. But he was none the less a real man. Are we to ask how one who was divine could also be human, or are we to ask how one who was human could also be divine? The traditional method has been in general to state the question in the first way. That is why it has never been able to do justice to Christ's humanity. Our thinking should begin with the known facts, not with a theory. What we know is that Jesus appeared in history as a human being who began life as we all begin it. What people saw in him, at least while he was on earth, was the characteristics of manhood. A few intimate friends, however, saw that the manhood was of a peculiar quality. Jesus said things, and did things, and made things possible, such as was true of no other. Within a few years of his death, thousands came to the same conclusion. In order to account for the facts as they understood them, they asserted his divinity. They believed that he had come from God on a mission to save the world, but they believed that because they had already had experience of his saving power.

The modern view is returning to this historical order. It recognizes that there are certain statements in the New Testament that suggest the "dogmatic" method, and deal with Jesus as though he were a divine being become human. But it insists that these statements must be looked at from the standpoint of the history. And the history presents us with, first, a man "like unto his brethren." Such statements must therefore be considered as explanatory and interpretative, and therefore as subject to criticism.

An increasing number of men are concerned to recover the historical and experiential facts which the later writings of the New Testament and the early creeds sought to explain and interpret. On one thing they insist: whatever else Jesus was or was not, he was a man. At the same time, it is just as clear that he was a certain kind of man: had he not been, we should never have had the history or the experience. He is a man who has shown the human race the way of its salvation. Both facts are to be taken into consideration: he was like us, yet he saves us. It is because of his saving power that we call him divine, but it is a divineness that can be predicated of a real human being.

A Teacher of Saving Truth. The modern view emphasizes Jesus' teaching function. The Word who became flesh was "full of truth." Men had wrong ideas about God, about themselves, about their relation to each other, and about their relation to God and his will. Jesus set himself to rectify these errors, and in our day that fact is coming into its own. He proclaimed God as Father and men as sons—rebellious sons, but none the less sons. The thought controlling all his utterance was that of the Family. He called it a Kingdom, but what he declared as the characteristics of the Kingdom—Fatherhood, sonship, brotherhood, and personal relations of trust and love and service— were rather the characteristics of a family than of any kingdom this world ever saw. He did not tell men that he had come to save them from God, but that he had come as God's messenger, God's prophet, God's son, to open to men the way of true life.

As was pointed out before, he was the living embodiment of his own message. He called men to a life of trust—and he trusted. He bade them serve—and he served. He warned them against sin—and he remained

sinless. He exalted sacrifice—and he sacrificed himself.
He stands forevermore a perfect and authenticating
expression of his own message of sacrificial love as the
world's supreme redemptive power. What he said about
God, about life, about salvation, must be true, because
he said it, and because in living it out he became what
he was.

We are realizing as never before this relation between
Jesus and his message, and between that message and
the world's salvation. We are seeing that the world
can be saved only in the way that was marked out by
Jesus—and that is a vastly more difficult way than by
merely subscribing to a creed. A man is saved only to
the extent to which he has the spirit of Jesus, which is
the spirit of filial love for God and fraternal love for
men. What the modern world is looking for is a way
of bringing the truth of Christ into the very centre of
its life and action.

Authoritative as to His Spirit. What has just been
said illustrates the sense in which alone the modern
view finds authority in Jesus. Whether the claim that
Jesus Christ is the world's Saviour is valid or not depends on just one thing—Is he really saving it? That
is to say, Is he destroying those influences that alienate
men from God and each other, and is he bringing love
where hate was, purity where uncleanness was, gentle-
ness where bitterness was, peace and good will and mutual regard where before was the spirit of strife? If he
is doing that, he is saving men in the only way in which
men need to be saved. It is useless to say that he "cannot" save unless he was this, that, or the other—unless, for example, he was born of a virgin, or unless he
worked miracles, or unless he had lived before the
worlds were made, or unless he went back to heaven

with the same body that was laid in the tomb. If he saves, then he has "saving power," and that in him which effects this salvation possesses an authority which cannot be overthrown.

What thus actually effects salvation is what we call his "spirit." A Christian is a man in whom is the spirit of Christ. This spirit is not an independent entity of some kind, which can be passed from person to person, like money. It is, as we shall see later, an attitude and quality of the inner life. A person has the spirit of Christ whose own spirit is Christlike, and there is no other way of having it. According as the Christlike spirit spreads in human affairs, there approaches that universal subjection of all things to Christ which is anticipated in the New Testament.

Herein is the authority of Jesus Christ for the mind of to-day. It is the authority of that spirit whose presence in the human heart saves the individual and whose triumph in all social life will mean the realization of the Kingdom of God. We do not need to assign authority to every word he said, or even to all his actions. As we saw before, he was a man of his own time. The spirit that was his expressed itself in such ways as the time made possible. The authority of the spirit does not necessarily pertain to all its forms of expression. We say all that needs to be said for the final truth and worth of the spirit of Christ when we say this—that if every man possessed it and exemplified it, there would come upon the world that blessedness and peace and joy which has ever been the world's desire.

An Original and Creative Moral Personality. We found that the Gospel portrayal of Jesus left us with an element of mystery. The recognition of that mystery remains in the modern view. Jesus is as big a problem to thought as he ever was. We still try to explain him, but we confess that there is an unexplainable remainder. There is something in every man which is not found in any other. The most satisfactory way to account for that unique element is by supposing that every time a new life comes into the world God does something he had never done before. He performs a new creative act. The character of the creation is conditioned by hereditary and environmental factors, because God is a God of law, and whatever he does he does in conditions that he himself prescribes. But the creativity is there none the less, and creation means not that God brings something out of nothing, but that he brings to expression out of the inexhaustible depths of his own being a hitherto unexpressed reality.

If we adopt this point of view, we can understand why Jesus Christ could be at once like us and unlike us. He was like us because he came into existence and remained in existence according to the same laws which make any human life possible—and this fact would not be affected by a miraculous conception, which has to do only with embryonic origin, not with embryonic processes or later environmental influences. He was unlike us as every man is unlike every other, except that in his case this unlikeness was such as to fit him to do something which none other was ever fitted to do. "God was in Christ." He is in every man in some sense, and according to that divine indwelling the man is able to do this or that work. God was in Plato—to make him a philosopher; in Shakespeare—to make him a poet; in Bach—to make him a musician; in Jesus Christ—to make him the supreme exponent of the religious life, the Author and Finisher of faith, the world's all-sufficient Saviour and Lord.

Jesus did as he did because he was as he was. What

made him as he was? God in him. Not that something is, so to speak, taken out of God and put in a man so that it then ceases to exist in God. But all that "truth and grace" which God eternally is, and which man must know and in which he must trust if he would find his true life—this we find in Jesus Christ. We find it there because God reveals it in the only way in which such truth and grace ever could be revealed, namely, in a human life which on its inward side is continuous with God and on its outward side is continuous with history. In such a personality there is at once the supernatural and the natural, or, more simply, the divine and the human.

Such a view does not make Jesus Christ any less Saviour or any less Lord than he ever was for men. It only strips away certain archaic wrappings from his Figure, and makes him more comprehensible to our mind.

X

THE HOLY SPIRIT

Few subjects connected with the Christian religion are more difficult than that of the Holy Spirit. The nature of this Spirit, the conditions and the method of its operation, the extent of its influence, and its relation to God on the one hand and to Christ on the other hand—these are questions which have been agitated for centuries. A good deal of bitterness has at times characterized the discussion. Men have thereby seemed to deny the very thing they were contending for. But we must not be led by this to lose sight of the real issue. Certain personal experiences were believed to be due ultimately to the direct influence of God himself. Many other questions have sprung from this central fact, but it is the central fact itself that we need always to keep in mind.

The General Idea of Spirit-Possession. The idea of spirit-possession is practically universal. The ecstatic state was known among all primitive people, as it still is, and the obvious explanation of ecstasy was that a spirit had taken possession of the man. The character of the spirit was inferred from the nature of the action to which the possessed person was led. Hence the spirit of jealousy, or of anger, or of revenge, or of madness; and at the other extreme, the spirit of wisdom, or of temperance, or of valor. Deliberate attempts were made to induce the ecstatic state—by drinking, by weird rites, by symbolic representations, by recitals, by violent physical exertion, by sudden excess following on a period of fasting and ritualistic ceremony. Often it was believed that the utterances of an ecstatic person were the utterances of the spirit or the god, to be heeded accordingly.

Complete passivity has also been regarded as a sign of spirit-possession. While in the passive state, the soul was believed to be in communication with the spirit-world. Both ecstasy and passivity have characterized the history of religion down into our own day, and may still be seen during periods of religious revival.

The Spirit in the Old Testament. There is no such thing in the Old Testament as a consistent doctrine of the divine Spirit. One reason for this is in the fact that men's ideas on the subject underwent continual change, as we should expect. Another reason is in the fact that the historical books of the Old Testament were composed at a later period than that of which they tell, and often reflect the language and ideas of the period of their composition.

There are many allusions to the Spirit in what might be called the *pre-prophetic* period. It rested upon the seventy elders of Moses (Num. 11 : 24–29). It fitted Joshua to succeed Moses (Num. 27 : 18). It accounted for the achievements of Othniel (Judges 3 : 10), of Gideon (Judges 6 : 34), of Samson (Judges 13 : 25), of Saul (I Sam. 11 : 6), and of David (I Chron. 28 : 12). There are also allusions to other spirits than the Spirit of God. These are the "evil spirits" (Judg. 9 : 23; I Sam. 16 : 14–23), and the "familiar spirits" (Lev. 19 : 31; I Sam. 28 : 3–7).

In the *prophetic* period, the teaching about the Spirit takes on a lofty ethical character. The written prophets, however, were preceded by a prophetic movement of the ecstatic type. There were "bands of prophets" who, by means of dancing and music, wrought themselves up to a high pitch of enthusiasm, and gave forth "prophesyings" which were attributed to the Spirit of God (I Sam. 10 : 5–11). The true and false mingled in these men (I Kings 13 : 18). In the case of Elijah and Elisha, however, there is much less of the merely ecstatic (cf. I Kings 19 : 9–14), and much more of the sense of a distinctly ethical vocation. "The word of the Lord" was spoken to them and by them (I Kings 17 : 2, 8, 16, 24), and they were recognized as peculiarly under the control of his Spirit (I Kings 18 : 12; II Kings 2 : 16).

These foreshadowings of a better understanding of the presence of God with men come to their fulfillment in the great prophets of Israel from the eighth to the fifth centuries B. C. From the days that Amos among the herdsmen of Tekoa heard the word of the Lord until the establishment of the theocratic state under Ezra and Nehemiah after the return from the Exile, there was a succession of men who believed themselves to speak under divine influence. Their common formula is, "The word of the Lord came to me." It usually came as a result of quiet brooding and contemplation (Isaiah 6; Hosea 1–3; but cf. Ezek. 8 and 11). The Spirit that they themselves possessed they believed it was God's purpose to "pour out" upon the nation (Ezek. 11 : 19, 20), and even upon all mankind (Joel 2 : 28–32), to make possible the life of true righteousness.

The Psalter is evidence to the fruitfulness of the prophets' teaching. The Psalter is the reflection of the spiritual life of Israel, as it was also one of the chief means whereby that life was nourished. The prophets far more than the priests were the creators of that vital personal piety, that deep longing after God, that cer-

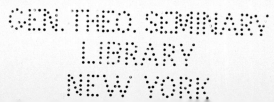

tainty of his presence and guidance, which are so characteristic of the Psalms. No people who did not have a rich experience of the divine presence could ever have produced these sacred poems; and no people who used them regularly in private and public worship could ever quite lose the sense of Immanuel—"God with us."

The *post-prophetic* period saw the written law made central. This exaltation of the letter inevitably checked the freedom of the spirit. The records of the past, and stated ritual acts, were placed between the soul and God. Attention, however, was directed to a future "day of the Lord," when the promise would be fulfilled, and "God would pour out his Spirit upon all flesh." This expectation is characteristic of Jewish thought in the centuries immediately preceding Christ.

The Spirit in the New Testament. The teaching here is just as complicated as it is in the Old Testament. We read different things in different places. Christianity soon came to include both Jews and Gentiles, and there are signs in the New Testament of the influence not only of the Jewish doctrine of the Spirit as a power sent from God upon men to comfort and guide and cleanse them, but also of the influence of the Greek idea of a universal World-Spirit, diffused through everything, and in which men must participate to find their true life.

Jesus and the Spirit. So far as we can learn from the first three Gospels (the Fourth Gospel will be considered separately), Jesus appears to have said little or nothing about the Spirit. The Spirit "over-shadowed" his mother before his birth (Luke 1 : 35). He was announced by John as one who would baptize with the Spirit (Luke 3 : 15–17). At his baptism by John, the Spirit visibly fell upon him (Matt. 3 : 16; cf. John 1 : 32–

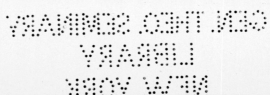

34). The Spirit was with him on his return from the temptation (Luke 4 : 14). And in the synagogue at Capernaum he deliberately claimed to be possessed of that same Spirit which had led Isaiah to preach "good tidings to the poor" (Luke 4 : 17 f.). Matt. 7 : 11 is much more likely to give Jesus' actual words than Luke 11 : 13. There is the difficult teaching about "the sin against the Holy Ghost" in Luke 12 : 10–12; and there is the Last Commission (Matt. 28 : 19), whose *form* many scholars believe to be unhistorical. These few references practically exhaust what Jesus said on the subject. It is a striking fact that one who was continually conscious of God's presence should have said so little about the Spirit. May it not be that in his own thought the Spirit and that continuous presence were one and the same thing?

The Spirit in the Acts. According to Luke, however, Jesus in his last interview with his disciples told them to wait at Jerusalem for the baptism of the Spirit (Acts 1 : 4, 5). The disciples interpreted their experience on the Day of Pentecost as both a fulfillment of the ancient promise and a vindication of their Lord (2 : 14–36). In the Acts the possession of the Spirit carries with it outward "signs" such as could not but impress the world (2 : 43); but it carries with it also an inward witness— righteousness, and peace, and joy. The Spirit became a guiding power in the lives of men, as when it led Philip to the Ethiopian eunuch (8 : 29), or as when it told Peter how to deal with the Gentile Cornelius (10 : 19), or as when it directed the church in the selection of Paul and Barnabas (13 : 2), or as when it kept Paul from going to Bithynia and instead opened the way to Macedonia (16 : 7). All the life and experience of the young Christian community were interpreted from the standpoint of Spirit-action and Spirit-possession. The Spirit comes of faith in Christ: it "falls on those that believe" (10 : 44).

The Spirit in Paul. It is impossible in a brief discussion to do justice to Paul's diverse and abundant teaching on the Spirit. As we meet him in the *Acts*, he shares the pervailing belief of the Christian community, namely, that the Spirit is a power given from God consequent on faith in Christ, whereby the believer may do signs and wonders to convince the world, and may have within himself a new spiritual life. Writing to the *Thessalonians*, he reminds them that he brought the Gospel to them "not in word only, but also in power, and in the Holy Spirit" (I Thess. 1 : 5). In *Corinthians* the ethical note is particularly strong. The Corinthian Christians were given to emotional excess, and Paul calls upon them to cultivate those other graces and virtues which more clearly distinguish the Christian from the worldly-minded. He would have all the life of their church animated by the Spirit, as the spirit of a man animates his body (I Cor. 12 : 4 f.). The power of the Spirit to bring freedom, especially freedom from the law and from the flesh, is the burden of much of Paul's teaching in *Galatians* (3 : 2; 5 : 16–25) and in *Romans* (8 : 1–16). In the latter passage, the Spirit is the law of a new life (verse 2); it promotes righteousness (10); it co-operates with man's own spirit (16); and it gives man power with God (26).

The idea in Corinthians that the church is the Body of Christ, of which the Spirit is the animating power, is elaborated in *Ephesians* and in *Colossians*. We are here told that God's purpose was to take all mankind, Jew and Gentile alike, and through Jesus Christ make of them one "household of God," in which God himself should dwell "in the Spirit" (Eph. 2 : 11–22; and cf. Col. 1 : 9 f.; 2 : 6 f.). Paul here shows a departure from the Jewish thought, and an approach to the Alexandrian, with its emphasis on an all-pervasive divine power and on an ideal unity of life. This power—what is it but the Holy Spirit? This unity—what is it but the life of the true Church?

A difficult question is as to how Paul relates the Spirit to Christ. Sometimes he speaks of them as though they were wholly separate; sometimes he identifies them; and sometimes he regards the Spirit as the Spirit *of* Christ, his own Spirit. It seems clear that Paul's thought on the subject underwent a radical change. He began with the ordinary Jewish doctrine of the Spirit as this was modified by the first disciples (see section above on Acts); but he eventually reached an interpretation of his own, namely, that the presence of the Spirit was the presence of Christ; that all that the Spirit was said to do, Christ himself did; that to be filled with the Spirit was to be filled with Christ; and that to live the life of the Spirit was to live a life hidden with Christ in God.

The Spirit in the Fourth Gospel. We find here a situation similar to what we find in Paul. There are places where John speaks of the Spirit in the accustomed way of the early church. See 1 : 32–33; 3 : 1–8; 4 : 20–24; 7 : 38, 39, and cf. 16 : 7. But how can we reconcile John the Baptist's declaration, "This is he that baptizeth in the Holy Spirit," with 7 : 39, "The Spirit was not yet given"? The difficulty is the more evident when we turn to chapters 14, 15, and 16. In these farewell discourses Jesus tells his disciples of experiences that will befall them after his death. He connects these experiences with one whom he calls "the Comforter"

(14 : 16), "the Spirit of truth" (14 : 17), "the Holy Spirit" (14 : 26), but whom he also seems to identify with himself (14 : 18, 28). The Comforter is the Father's gift (14 : 26), yet it is also the Son's gift (15 : 26). Both Father and Son will come and dwell with the man who loves the Son (14 : 23), and Jesus anticipates a union thus described: "I in them, and thou in me, that they may be perfected into one" (17 : 23).

Moreover, much of the teaching of the Fourth Gospel bears on the new life that may come to men who accept Jesus and his word. He is presented as himself the Light, who came to give men light; the Life, who came to give men life; the Truth, who came to give men truth. To believe in him is to have everlasting life. To accept the truth he brings is to be set free. To eat his flesh and drink his blood is to abide in him, and have him abide in oneself.

It is hardly possible to deduce from this diverse teaching a consistent doctrine of the mutual relations of Father, Son, Holy Spirit, and believer. We can only suggest that in places John reports the ordinary belief about the Spirit as a sort of half-physical substance that can be "poured out," "given," and "taken away," but that he also has a different belief of his own. This belief resembles that of Paul on his mystical side, namely, that what was ordinarily regarded as the presence and action of the Spirit in the Christian community was in reality the presence and action of Christ himself.

The Church Doctrine of the Holy Spirit. When the Church of the early centuries entered upon its theologizing activity, it found itself in possession of the diverse teaching briefly outlined above. For a long time men had been satisfied simply to use the various Scriptural expressions. It was inevitable, however, that with the three terms, Father, Son, and Holy Spirit, in constant use, the question of their deeper relations would be raised. The problem seems not to have been an urgent one at the Council of Nicæa (325 A. D.). The Nicene Creed says simply: "And I believe in the Holy Spirit." It was a group of fourth-century thinkers known as the Cappadocian theologians (Gregory of Nyssa, Gregory Nazianzen, and Basil of Cesaræa), who definitely took the step of affirming the full divinity and personality of the Holy Spirit, as the third of a trinity of co-equal and co-eternal Divine Persons. Each person had his own characteristics. The Father is the basic fact, the Unbegotten; the Son is generated or begotten of the Father; and from the Father proceeds the Holy Spirit. They are all of one and the same substance, and neither alone is God, but God consists of the three persons in their eternal corporate life. The Council of Constantinople (381 A. D.) added to the Nicene Creed this doctrine of the procession and divinity of the Spirit. In 589 A. D. the Synod of Toledo affirmed that the Spirit proceeded from *both* Father and Son. The Eastern Church refused to accept the addition, and the controversy was one of the causes of the division of the Church into Greek Catholic and Roman Catholic.

The Doctrine of the Holy Spirit an Attempt to Interpret Experience. The various assertions, Scriptural and theological, about the Holy Spirit, rest ultimately upon an experience and the desire to account for it. Men knew certain things about themselves to be true. They knew that a sudden access of strength came to them. They knew that they felt repentance and remorse for wrong-doing. They knew that old and evil desires passed away, and that new and good desires took their place. They knew that they had an inward peace and joy which no outward circumstance could disturb. They knew that dark things at last became clear, that wisdom was granted to them in times of crisis, that they were enabled to bear the ills of life, and that the very things that seemed to threaten their faith could be turned into means whereby that faith was strengthened. They saw great social changes taking place, legislation becoming more humane, despotisms falling to pieces, institutions coming into existence to promote human good.

All this men observed, and they were constrained to account for it. They realized that the human will was involved in all such experiences, but they believed that there was something else besides. What engendered in the human mind the new ideas? What brought the will to the place where the new ideas could be made operative? Men answered their questions by asserting the activity of the Divine Spirit. It was God by his Spirit who made possible these rich and varied personal and social experiences. There were many variations and refinements of this general answer, and these are often enough confusing to the mind, but through it all the reality of the experiences and the reasonableness of the general answer remain.

The Problem of Re-interpretation. There are many people for whom the traditional doctrine of the Holy Spirit is no longer convincing, who yet are firmly convinced of the reality of their experience of God. Any attempt at re-interpretation will therefore mean for such people simply a new understanding of the conditions whereby man comes to his apprehension of God. All that men have ever meant by the Holy Spirit can be expressed in one simple phrase, "God-with-us."

There are many grades of the experience, because the experience itself is under law. If we could learn that law, and fulfill it perfectly, then we could have a perfect experience of the Holy Spirit, which is the same as saying that we could be in perfect relationship with God. Whatever a man does or feels under a conviction of the divine will is for him an experience of the Holy Spirit. It is God reaching him in the only way in which God ever can reach any one, and it is the man knowing God in the only way in which it is possible to know him. God may, of course, seek to reach a man and evoke no response whatever. This divine seeking may still be regarded as the action of the Holy Spirit, but, after all, it is only because some men have actually found God that there is reason to believe that he is seeking others. It is therefore only the completed experience that is really significant. When the experience is complete, we can then analyze it to ascertain its conditions, and we can see that if man finds God it is because he is already *able* to find him and because God is already *seeking* him. What has led men to believe in the Holy Spirit is not merely a conviction that God seeks them, but the realization that he finds them and they find him.

This is the fact that is calling for re-interpretation. The Holy Spirit is, so to speak, a divine-human fusion. It is man knowing God, and God entering into the life of man. There are therefore two questions to be asked: (1) What are the human conditions to man knowing God? Here we find the need for various instrumentalities—nature, social contacts, art, music, literature, and other forms of human achievement; for definite religious instruction; for personal belief and faith, especially in relation to Jesus Christ. All this assumes on man's part a fundamental capacity for God. (2) What are the divine conditions to God entering into the life of man? The traditional Christian answer to this question involves the doctrine of the Trinity, as stated above. Much that has been said about the Trinity would seem to suppose that there are three distinct and separate Gods. One of these is the Holy Spirit, whose function it is to act for the Godhead in its purpose to influence human life. There are many indications that this explanation is becoming increasingly unsatisfactory. But the trinitarian formula reveals a sound instinct for fact—fact which those who surrender the formula will still have to recognize and protect. If there is in man a capacity for God, which is presupposed in the God-with-man experience, then there must be on God's part a capacity for man. *This divine capacity for man, or, more exactly, this power on the part of God to enter into the life of men, is what we mean by the Holy Spirit on its so-called objective side.* God is still that kind of God, even though men should utterly ignore him. That is why we shall continue to speak of the Holy Spirit as divine, as eternal, as an essential element in the total Christian conception of God.

XI

JESUS CHRIST AND THE CHURCH

The church and its history are parts of the total facts connected with the Christian religion, and if we are to understand what the Christian religion is, we must take the church and its history into consideration. There is doubtless a great difference between the church as it came to be and the thought of Jesus concerning the growth of his work. Nevertheless, the historical church shows to a large extent how the Christian religion has actually worked in human life, and for that reason the history is significant.

Did Jesus Found the Church? The answer to the question is Yes. Jesus did not found the church in the sense that the vast organization such as afterwards appeared fulfilled in all respects his original plan and purpose. But he did found it in the sense that this organization arose out of the work he did, the message he proclaimed, the impulses that he set free, and the convictions that he created in men's minds.

The Gospels afford ample evidence that Jesus' main purpose was to bring a new spirit into human life, resulting from a new relation of men to God, and manifesting itself in a new relation of men to each other. He came to bring in the Kingdom of God, but we can hardly identify the Kingdom as he conceived it with the organized church of later years. He is alleged to have instituted the sacraments of Baptism and the Lord's Supper, but it is uncertain whether he gave them the significance that they presently came to have.

Many scholars, indeed, believe that the words of the Last Commission (Matt. 28 : 19) were put into the mouth of Jesus by those who wished to claim his sanction for later ecclesiastical practice. But even if this be not so, there is little reason for believing that he regarded the baptismal act in a distinct sacerdotal way. The experience of the two disciples at Emmaus, to whom the Risen Christ made himself known in the breaking of the bread at their ordinary evening meal, was at least one possible fulfillment of Jesus' idea at the Last Supper. So far as the records go, Jesus used the term "church" only twice, Matt. 16 : 18 and 18 : 17. In the second case the context makes it clear that church "means the little community of Jewish Christians" (Streeter). In the first case, the words to Peter —"upon this rock will I build my church"—we have a much more difficult problem. Roman Catholicism builds upon it much of its claim for the supremacy of the Pope. Most Protestants hold that the Roman claim gives a meaning to the words of Jesus far other than their original intention: the rock upon which Jesus would build was not Peter himself, but *Peter's confession of the Divine Sonship*. The question is one that cannot be settled by exegesis: it will be settled rather by the preconceptions of the interpreter. Whatever the interpretation, however, it will still remain that Jesus said he would found his church. What did he mean by "church"? Evidently some kind of organization, of which the disciples whom he had so carefully trained would be the nucleus and the natural leaders. Otherwise, he would be leaving the carrying on of his work to chance, and all that John believed he meant by the Holy Spirit precludes the supposition that he would do this.

The facts in the case are that Jesus created a fellowship, the bond of which was devotion to himself and faith in his words, and that he laid upon this fellowship of believing men the obligation of self-increase, and instructed them as to their procedure. In this sense he founded the church, because the church of history actually began with this fellowship. These facts, however, need not prevent us from accepting the results of historical study, which leave little doubt that the *form* actually taken by the church was partly determined by psychological and social and even economic factors.

The Beginnings of the Organized Church. The opening chapters of the Acts describe the beginnings of the church. What we see there can be called an organization in only a very accommodated sense. Even the few ecclesiastical features that are present are undoubtedly exaggerated through being described from the standpoint of the succeeding generation, when the ecclesiastical idea was beginning to form. The original church was really a brotherhood—at the most a religious society. It is significant that Luke says that the instructions given to the disciples by the Risen Christ concerned "the Kingdom of God": he does not say the church (Acts 1 : 3). The disciples were commissioned to be witnesses to Christ in all the world (1 : 8), and nothing is said, as in the Last Commission in Matthew, even of baptizing. They were a band of praying men and women (1 : 14), waiting to be endued with power (1 : 8). They believed they were to exercise a ministry and an apostleship, and that they had the right to choose one of their number to take the place of Judas, but they made the choice of Matthias (1 : 26) for just one reason —that he might be a witness to the resurrection (1 : 22). Peter's sermon on Pentecost led to a great enlargement of the group, but the description of the life of this large body is still that of a simple religious brotherhood. It is true that there was baptism, instruction, fellowship, a common meal (apparently in addition to the ordinary meal of the homes), and worship, but the keynote of the description is extreme simplicity (2 : 42–47). Each helped the other as he could, but there was no thought of a separatist movement. The Christians were still "Jews, devout men" (2 : 5), who "continued steadfastly with one accord in the temple" (2 : 46). The authorities soon began to be disturbed, not, however, because of any corporate aspect of the brotherhood, but because of the ideas it was spreading. Hence the injunction to Peter and John was not to disband a dangerous organization, but to "speak no more nor teach in the name of Jesus" (4 : 18). A certain priority and authority was assigned to the Twelve because of their intimate personal association with the Lord in the days of his flesh (4 : 35, 37), but there are as yet no other ecclesiastical indications. "The whole church" of 5 : 11 was simply the large body of men and women in Jerusalem who had accepted the apostles' testimony to Jesus Christ. It even included "a great company of the priests" (6 : 7), who apparently still continued to exercise their office in the temple.

The Appearance of Ecclesiasticism. This simple religious society, however, soon began to realize the need of a closer organization. This arose partly from growth in numbers, partly from the desire to keep in touch with each other following the dispersion of the Jerusalem group by persecution, and partly from the growing missionary zeal. The "election" and "ordination" of seven men to administer charity, and thereby give the apostles more time for specifically religious work, took place while the believers were still in Jerusalem (6 : 1–7).

It is significant that at about this time the Jewish leaders began to see in the Christian community a possible rival organization (6 : 11–14), a fact which led to the martyrdom of Stephen and the scattering of believers. Because of this dispersion Philip came to Samaria, and there preached Christ to good effect. Peter and John came down from Jerusalem to see his work. They laid their hands upon the converts, who thereupon "received the Holy Spirit" (8 : 14–17). Here we see the beginnings of *the extension of apostolic authority*, and the belief that through the laying on of the apostles' hands a peculiar grace might come to men.

From this point on in the story there are increasing signs that the Christian community is becoming, so to speak, self-conscious. Its interests become more complex. Men of diverse gifts enter its fellowship. A division of labor is set up. The conception of a world-wide mission emerges. The community becomes troubled by serious problems—problems of procedure, problems of relation to the older religion, problems of discipline, problems arising from the jealousies of leaders. By the missionary zeal of refugees and of those deliberately sent out for the purpose, the community establishes itself in many centres. This calls for oversight, and the maintenance of the relation of group to group. Instruction becomes necessary, especially for those who are won from paganism, and a teaching order is established. If there are teachers, there must be something to be taught, and this tends to encourage doctrinal formulation, a process further accelerated by the necessity of the community to protect itself against alien influences. The conditions of membership become more exacting. The common meal or "love feast" gives way to the specific celebration of the Lord's Supper at stated times.

Before we are out of the pages of the New Testament, therefore, we have ample evidence that the brotherhood of faith and love created by Jesus has developed into an *ecclesia* or church, with doctrines, sacraments, varying grades of officials, such as bishops, elders, deacons, prophets, teachers, evangelists, with a consciousness of the unity of its various parts in a corporate life, and with a disposition to claim that through it alone could salvation be found.

The Spirit of Christ and Church Form. In all this the church believed it was led by the Spirit of its Lord. But this divine leading was determined to some extent by circumstances. We know the form that the church actually took. But what we cannot say is that it was that form or none, or that the original form is binding on Christian men for ever. It has yet to be shown that the many variant forms of church organization were not as truly possessed of the Spirit of Christ as was the alleged original form. The episcopal churches and the non-episcopal churches, the churches which emphasize ritual and those which emphasize preaching, have no occasion to dispute as to which is right or wrong. The Spirit of Christ has been as manifest in one form as in the other. There is just one test of the validity of any church organization, procedure, or practice, namely, in how far does it promote the work of Christ in the world ? "Where the Spirit of Christ is, there is the catholic church."

The Church According to Augustine. The movement toward the conception of the church as a great hierarchy, with divinely bestowed authority over the minds and souls of men, came to its climax in Augustine (354–430 A. D.), who gave the sanction of his great name to the doctrine, which already had been frequently set forth by earlier theologians, that outside the church there is no salvation. That would have been a profound truth if Augustine had consistently maintained the distinction between "the church visible and the church invisible." He does, indeed, allow the distinction, but only to affirm that some in the visible church may not belong to the church invisible, never to affirm that membership in the church invisible can be reached in any other way than through the church visible.

We have here the so-called catholic idea of the church, and it has continued until this day. History attests both its weakness and its strength. There is no need to dispute that at certain times and for certain purposes it has been indispensable. But that is not to say that it is entirely true. There were, in fact, many "sects" in the fourth and fifth centuries—groups of Christians organized on a different basis from that which ordinarily prevailed. Protestantism was largely a "protest" against the catholic idea of the church. Denominationalism is simply the Protestant principle run wild, but the principle itself is not thereby invalidated. What is needed is a way of avoiding mere denominationalism on the one hand, and on the other hand the literal *identifying* of "the church which is his Body" with any given form of organization.

The Church and the Churches. Paul conceived the church as the Body of Christ, of which individuals are organic parts (Eph. 3:1–4:16; I Cor. 12:4–28). By this he meant the universal community of the saved, and for this purpose he defined salvation as the possession of the Spirit of Christ. But he also spoke of the church in the narrower sense of a given group of Christians viewed as having a common religious experience and purpose (I Cor. 1:2; 16:19; Col. 4:15, 16). This distinction we must still make, except that to-day the differences between the given groups are much more pronounced than anything that was possible in Paul's time. Many of these differences are coming to have only an historical interest, but there is no immediate prospect of their altogether disappearing. Perhaps this is just as well. Human nature being as it is, one universal world-wide organization would be in serious danger of becoming arrogant.

But, although we may assume the continuance of different ecclesiastical organizations, we do not need to assume the continuance of their rivalry. Indeed, one of the encouraging features of our time is the tendency to replace rivalry with co-operation. The churches of to-day are realizing that they are confronted with a much greater task than that of dwelling upon and perpetuating their differences. Instead of challenging each other's right to be called a church because of theological, sacramentarian, ritualistic, or ecclesiastical differences, they are beginning to turn their attention to the question of what *any* church is in the world to do. To that question there can finally be but one answer: to cultivate, exhibit, and propagate the Spirit of Christ. Men may differ as to what this involves: that gives us "churches." But through all the differences there runs the common purpose to make Christ Lord, and the total number of those who have this purpose gives us "The Church."

"The Church" Outside the Churches. The church in its universal sense is more than the total number of the churches. Indeed, one of the facts that the churches must seriously consider is their inability to appeal to men and women of a certain type who yet in their whole spirit and bearing show that they are seeking to exemplify the mind of Christ. On the other hand, such people are suffering from their own aloofness, and limiting their own social effectiveness. They need what comes from Christian fellowship, and others need what they are able to contribute. It is still true that the organized churches are the most effective instruments for spreading in the world the Spirit of Jesus Christ, and thereby promoting the Kingdom of God.

The Church and Other Organizations. The churches are not the only instruments of the Spirit of Christ. There are a great number of other organizations, all of which seek to advance that Kingdom of God for which Jesus lived and died. But it is significant that the fruitful mother of these organizations is the church itself. They provide for many, especially for "the church outside the churches," a channel for self-expression, but there are limitations on their scope and purpose which make them religiously inadequate. They *express* the Spirit of Christ rather than *cultivate* the definitely inward aspects of the Christian life. They direct power rather than generate it. They have no sanctuary for the soul. They reach outward rather than upward. They seek to bring in a better social order rather than to cultivate the sense of the eternal that God has set in the heart of man, or the sense of personal relation to his Lord which is the secret of the Christian's joy and the source of his moral strength. The value of these organizations is immense, but they are not churches, and the real work of the churches they cannot do.

The Church in Mission Lands. A realization of the extent to which the church of history has been determined by psychological and social forces should relieve us from all anxiety as to the future of the church in those lands in which Christianity has been but recently established. What we can be sure of is that Oriental culture, for example, will provide from within itself the forms by which it will express its understanding of the mind of Christ. It is very certain that if early Christianity had not developed in the Roman Empire it would not have taken the form it did. Christianity itself is universal, but there should be *congruity* between the "culture" of a given people and that people's statements of dogma, forms of worship, and organized life as Christian. It may well be that an "imported" church form is necessary in that early period when the Christian community is being created in the new land; but as the Christian community comes to self-consciousness, it is inevitable that deep-seated national characteristics, which are matters not of choice but of social and psychological heritage, will manifest themselves in religious expression. The missionary needs the support of a denomination: that is a simple matter of strategy. But his aim is not to extend the denomination. Rather is it to extend the reign of Christ. In doing that, he may create a Christian community that will eventually want to go its own way. That need alarm nobody. The same Divine Spirit in the heart of men that has wrought with social and psychological forces in the past to give the church its form will continue to work in the same way in the future.

Men must speak and hear spoken "in their own language" the wonderful works of God. The continuity of the historic church is not a continuity of dogma, or of ritual, or of government. Instead, it is a continuity of faith, of purpose, of experience. Christ prayed that those who were to come to believe on him "might all be one." The unity he was thinking of was, indeed, an organic unity, but it was organic not as to external machinery but as to internal life and spirit.

XII

THE LIFE ETERNAL

The belief in some form of immortality has been practically universal. In our own day a great many people are claiming scientific evidence for the belief. On the other hand, there is probably more *questioning* of the belief at present than at any time in the past. The denial is being assisted by certain forms of the theory of evolution, and especially by the psychological theory which regards man as merely a complicated machine. Even religious people are claiming that immortality may be given up, and the belief in God and the life of fellowship with him still be retained. It is, however, impossible to give a complete statement of Christianity without including the affirmation of eternal life.

Immortality in the Old Testament. The early Hebrews shared the general belief in an underworld, or Sheol—the Hades of Greek thought—as the abode of the departed. But they thought of it as more or less disconnected with the present life, and as lying beyond the jurisdiction of Jehovah. Many scholars believe that for early Hebrew thought man was not body *and* soul in the sense of two wholly distinct and separate things temporarily held together, but a living whole distinguishable as body and soul. At death, the soul did not continue to live a complete life elsewhere, since without the body it was a "shade," a mere relic of what had once been. In the fate of this relic or shade the living had little interest.

The real interest of the early Hebrews was in the continuity of his own family. As the family continued, he also continued. In his posterity he could be rewarded, and in his posterity he could be punished. Hence the intense desire for a large family: it guaranteed the persistence of the "name" of the household (Gen. 15–18). In the early development of the messianic hope, this conception was applied to the nation. It was the *nation* that was to endure. The Messiah was to reign for ever, not over the same subjects, but over a succession of subjects that would never fail.

Those changes in the national life and experience which led to the break-up of the Jewish state in the Exile forced a reconsideration of the whole question. Indications begin to appear of a growing faith in individual persistence. Jehovah's purpose with man does not end at death: there is a future other than the corporate future (Psalms 73 : 23–26; 139 : 7–12; Job 19 : 25–27). Out of the same change in the national life came Ezekiel's doctrine of the individual, a doctrine which further emphasized the possibility of the relation of man to God remaining unbroken through death.

It is significant that from this time on in Hebrew thought immortality appears more and more as a *religious* truth—a truth, that is, arising out of the character of God and his righteous purpose. The way of the ungodly is to perish, and the way of the righteous is to endure, because God is what he is—holy and righteous. There is, however, a limitation on the conception, due chiefly to the Hebrew inability to think of life except under bodily conditions. There must be a *restoration of the body* in order to have fulness of life. At first, as in Ezek. 37 : 1–14, and Isaiah 26 : 19, the dead whose bodies are to be restored are the dead of righteous Israel (cf. Isaiah 26 : 14); but by the second century before Christ there is a definite doctrine of universal resurrection, of both good and evil (Daniel 12 : 2). The abundant Jewish literature of this same period and later, which is not included in the Old Testament, is full of this belief in a "day of the Lord" when all the dead shall leave their graves and receive their just rewards.

By the time of Christ, therefore, there was in Israel a well-defined doctrine of immortality and resurrection. It was for the most part stated under sensuous pictorial forms: immortality for the righteous is life on a rejuvenated earth; for the unrighteous it is life in a place of shadows and afflictions.

The Teaching of Jesus. The report of Jesus' teaching on immortality is so often associated with his "second coming" that we can never be quite sure to what extent his own words were colored by the presuppositions and prejudices of those who reported him. What we know is that he lived at a time when men were expecting a great cataclysm to usher in the day of the Lord and the blessed reign of the Messiah. To what extent Jesus himself accepted this view we shall never know with certainty, although he is represented as using frequently the highly pictorial language in which the view was expressed.

What is likely is that Jesus spoke concerning the future at different times in two radically different ways. He spoke of it sometimes after the manner of the accepted Jewish eschatology (Matt. 10 : 28–33; 18 : 7–14; 19 : 27–30; 24; 25; and the parallels). Here we have brought together such ideas as those of a sudden manifestation of God, resurrection, the appearance of Messiah, the endless doom of the wicked, and the endless bliss of the righteous. But Jesus sometimes spoke of the future in a very different way from this. He spoke of eternal life as a gift of God, and he defined this life as an abiding consciousness of the divine presence, an experience beginning here and now for those who accepted the truth and who cultivated faith and love, and an experience that nothing could destroy, not even death. The first type of teaching predominates in the Synoptic Gospels, the second type in the Fourth Gospel. Yet the more spiritual conception is also found in the earlier Gospels, as the more material conception is in the later Gospel. The probabilities are, therefore, that Jesus used both forms of teaching, but because the apocalyptic form better fitted in with the disciples' wishes and hopes, it was given the prominent place in the early Gospel tradition. The other form of teaching, however, still persisted. Experience more and more tended to emphasize and confirm this form, and to call in question the other, at least in its literal interpretation. The author of the Fourth Gospel, writing late in the first century, takes advantage of the situation, and presents almost exclusively the spiritual side of Jesus' teaching concerning eternal life. This side certainly agrees the better with the Gospel portrayal of Jesus as a whole. It is too much to ask us to believe that he was the victim of a false outlook, and that he made predictions about himself and his kingdom that were never to be fulfilled.

The Teaching of Paul. Paul's teaching shows affinities with both aspects of the teaching in the four Gospels. What is significant, however, is the fact that the more material form of the teaching is found in his earliest writings, and that he appears finally to have given this up altogether in the interests of the more spiritual form. Paul's earliest letters are those to the Thessalonians, and in both of them, but especially in the second, the whole idea of the coming of Christ to the accompaniment of resurrection and judgment is set forth in the fashion of the eschatological discourses of the Synoptic Gospels. "For the Lord himself shall descend from heaven, with a shout, with the voice of the archangel," etc. (I Thess. 4 : 13–18). Christ is to be "revealed from heaven with the angels of his power in flaming fire . . . when he shall come to be glorified in his saints" (II Thess. 1 : 5 f., and cf. 2 : 1–12). We can easily understand why these ideas should be present in Paul's earlier Christian thinking. He had, as a Pharisee, been trained in literalistic theories of resurrection, and he simply tried at first to fit his new beliefs concerning Christ into the old framework. But he gradually came to a more spiritual view, as he did also in the case of his doctrine of the scope of the Gospel and his doctrine of the Holy Spirit. His more matured thinking he sets forth in such passages as I Cor. 15; II Cor. 5 : 1–10; Phil. 3 : 20, 21. He here still associates resurrection and immortality. In doing this, he is true to his Jewish heritage. But he is also familiar with the speculative difficulties—especially as these appeared to the Greek mind—connected with the idea of bodily resurrection, and he has, moreover, surrendered his hope of living until the Lord's return.

Paul, however, cannot think of immortality except as there is resurrection. He finds his clue in the resurrection of Christ. That Christ rose again he regards as an absolute fact, and it carries with it the certainty of the resurrection of those who love him. But with the same body as before? No. Christ's own resurrection body was different from the body of his flesh. Things possible to the one body were not possible to the other. Yet the resurrection body was just as *real* as the earthly body. The body of a bird is different from the body of a man, yet each is a body, and it does what is required of it. The resurrection body is not *like* the earthly body, but it is none the less a body. Each is the instrument of the same spirit, and it differs because the needs of the spirit differ. But for the body of the tomb there would not be the body of glory. Both bodies are related through a common spirit, and this relation is compatible with the most profound differences. It is therefore no disembodied existence that Paul contemplates, but a rich and satisfying life of increased powers and activities—a glorified existence of which the resurrection life of Christ is the type.

Immortality for All Alike. Are immortality and resurrection the prerogatives only of those who have faith in Christ? This is not the thought of a single writer of the New Testament. In the Synoptic Gospels, mankind is divided into the righteous and the wicked, and a future existence awaits them both. In the teaching of Paul, judgment with ensuing rewards and penalties is to be accorded to all mankind. In the Fourth Gospel, eternal life has its correlative in eternal death, but both terms are qualitative: the one refers to life with God, the other to life without God. In the Revelation of John, the final conflict between the powers of good and the powers of evil is to end in the complete victory of the good, but the evil are to know that they are defeated, and they can know it only as they continue in conscious existence.

There is the further question of incomplete and subnormal personalities, and of those vast numbers who have passed out of life with no real knowledge of God and with little enough opportunity to acquire any. The whole subject is full of perplexities and difficulties. Some seek refuge in a theory of *annihilation* for all such as are eventually found not worthy to survive. Others regard immortality as *conditional* on a certain moral quality of the present life, and those who are unable or unwilling to meet the condition simply pass out of existence at death. Others anticipate the time of *universal restoration*—the final and complete salvation of every soul that God ever made. It is a place where dogmatism is impossible. What is certain is that Christ believed he had everlasting significance for all mankind. He revealed God as a Father of infinite love, who created men for endless fellowship with himself, and who would exhaust all his resources in order to win them. That the incident of physical death should irrevocably fix human character and destiny seems to many to be quite out of keeping with the idea of a Father-God and with the transformable quality of human nature. The final enthronement of Christ in every human soul, though it take ages and long travail to accomplish it, is surely a more worthy consummation of creation than a final universe in which evil shall have a permanent place. This view does not encourage moral indifference, nor justify the expectation that God will at last save all men whether they will or not. We have to take account of the law of habit, whereby the farther a man wanders from God the more difficult is the return, the more searching the penitence, the more prolonged the self-abasement, the more poignant the memories. That will be just as true in a future life as it is in the present.

Immortality Necessarily Individual. In modern times there has been a reversion to the idea of "social" immortality which we saw characterized early Hebrew thought. We are being told that the only way in which our life can continue is according as we build it into the lives of others. Not only is this said to be the only way in which immortality can be made intelligible; it is even said to be the only immortality that is desirable.

As a matter of fact, however, it is not intelligible at all. "Social immortality" is really a meaningless phrase. Immortality does not mean merely the influence exerted by one life upon another. It means rather the deathlessness of the human spirit, and the only way in which the human spirit can be deathless is by its retaining its self-consciousness. To live on, but not to know it, is the same as not living on. Character cannot continue if the person who created it does not continue.

Moreover, the alleged "social immortality" turns out, on closer consideration, to be doomed to end. The individual lives on, so we are told, only in society. The values or disvalues that he achieves are conserved in other lives. The same thing holds good of these other lives: they also live on in others in their turn. But even this process is not endless. It would be endless only if the human race were to go on reproducing itself forever. Yet the one certain thing is that the human race is doomed. There was a time when the earth could not support life, and that time will come again. The earth is mortal, and the life it nourishes and sustains is mortal. If values *must be* conserved, it can only be as the life is conserved in which values are realized. Even the much-lauded "social values" depend upon individual men and women, and if all individuals should cease to be, all social values would cease to be also.

The denial of individual immortality therefore presents us with the prospect of the time inevitably coming when everything for which men lived and worked and died shall utterly cease to be. The last word of materialism is an unrelieved pessimism. On the other hand, individual immortality means that nothing will finally perish. It means that we are "pilgrims of the infinite." It means that the law of the harvest is not confined in its operation to the here and now. It means that a vast and solemn significance attaches to every human soul. It means that we are storing up in the present life an equipment of habit and purpose and attitude which, for good or ill, we shall perforce carry with us into a life to come.

Christianizing the Present World-Order. It goes without saying that Christ's complete triumph is a question of the remote future. But it is false to infer from this that Christ has no particular significance for men in the world that now is, but only in the world that is to come. Certainly no interpretation of Christianity is adequate which does not relate Christ and the faithful soul in an everlasting companionship. But neither is any interpretation adequate which supposes that that companionship is not to be made effective in the present world.

In the New Testament the Kingdom is represented as both present and future, as both visible and invisible, as both "on the earth" and "in heaven," as both a new inner life and a new world-order. The future of the Kingdom of God on the earth is just as urgent a problem as the future of the Kingdom of God beyond the earth. How long the human race will continue, nobody knows. But it is evident that the race has a destiny here just as truly as the individual soul has a destiny hereafter. It is not enough that through our faith in Christ we can look forward without fear to whatever may be awaiting us individually after death. There is also the continuing life of mankind upon the earth to-day and to-morrow. Can we make it Christian? That is to say, Can we hope to embody the Spirit of Christ more and more in human relationships? There is no greater question. For if that be not possible, then the outlook is black indeed.

Consider the situation. Social life is becoming increasingly complex. Nature is yielding up her secrets with ever-increasing rapidity. The possibility of a universal cataclysm in which civilization shall destroy itself grows every day more real. What can save mankind from perishing of its own achievements? One thing only—the enthronement of Jesus Christ as King of Kings and Lord of Lords.

But such an enthronement will not be a merely negative thing. Christ will not simply stave off ruin: he will bring a positive salvation. If he could have his way with men, there would be no industrial oppression, no hopeless little children, no cheerless old age, no grinding poverty, no fattening of the few on the toil of the many, no racial hatreds, no armaments, no false standards of judgment as between man and man Only as the race can make progress in this direction can there be any hope of the future, and such progress depends entirely on whether or not the followers of Jesus Christ are willing to leave the eternal fate of their souls in their Lord's hands while they devote themselves to the task of making his Spirit operative in the world of to-day.

APPENDIX

APPENDIX

I

BIBLIOGRAPHY, AND SUGGESTIONS FOR FURTHER READING

The most that could be done in a brief treatment like the present was to state in broad outline the most essential of the Christian beliefs, and to offer some explanation of their meaning. The student who has mastered this little book may consider himself prepared for more extensive reading and study. A really comprehensive and scientific knowledge of Christianity calls for many years of patient study, for the problems raised are complex, and the literature of the subject is inexhaustible. The student, however, does not need to be discouraged, for the study, be it little or much, brings its own great rewards and satisfactions, and one treads with a firmer step as one goes on.

The study of the Christian religion and its beliefs follows roughly a threefold division, described technically as Biblical Theology, History of Doctrines, and Systematic Theology. The first endeavors to give an orderly account of the teaching of the Scriptures on the various questions with which theology deals. The second gives an account of the doctrines of Christianity in general, and of the doctrines of the different church bodies, as these were formulated in the first place, and as they may have been modified from time to time. The third is the effort of individual men to take the Christian beliefs and doctrines, and by the help of a certain philosophy combine them into a well-ordered and consistent whole.

The choice of books in these three fields is almost endless. The following may be recommended as being easily obtainable and not too technical.

Biblical Theology. H. Wheeler Robinson, "The Religious Ideas of the Old Testament" (Scribners); G. B. Stevens, "The Theology of the New Testament" (Scribners). The first of these is brief, but it is readable and dependable. The second is much larger; it is lucid in style, reverent and scholarly in treatment, and in the best sense conservative and evangelical.

History of Doctrines and of Christian Thought. Most of the reliable treatments in this field, such as Hagenbach, Dorner, Loofs, Harnack, and Seeberg, are too elaborate for the non-specialist. The student would probably get most help if he began with A. V. G. Allen, "The Continuity of Christian Thought" (Houghton, Mifflin and Co.). This is a book from a former generation, but it is a classic in both style and content. Somewhat different in character are H. B. Workman, "Christian Thought to the Reformation" (Scribners), not exhaustive but quite reliable, and A. C. McGiffert, "The Rise of Modern Religious Ideas" (Macmillan), a brilliant study, but in some respects radical. More pretentious works are H. C. Sheldon, "History of Christian Doctrine," 2 vols., revised (Abingdon Press), and G. P. Fisher, "History of Christian Doctrine" (Scribners), both excellent for reference purposes.

Systematic Theology. There is still no better single volume than W. N. Clarke, "An Outline of Christian Theology" (Scribners). It is spiritual, constructive, and evangelical, and has held a leading place for a generation. Somewhat more formal, and giving more attention to the Biblical and historical material, is W. A. Brown, "Christian Theology in Outline" (Scribners). Two more recent books that can be highly commended are W. F. Tillett, "Paths That Lead to God" (Doran), especially valuable for its copious extracts from the literature of the subject, and A. E. Garvie, "The Christian Doctrine of the Godhead" (Doran), a book which covers a wider field than the title suggests, and while somewhat diffuse in style is scholarly, and breathes a warm evangelical spirit.

In addition to these general treatments, the student should acquaint himself with a few of the books that deal more specifically with particular questions, such as the following:

Meaning of Religion. D. M. Edwards, "The Philosophy of Religion" (Doran). Sir Henry Jones, "A Faith That Enquires" (Macmillan). W. R. Matthews, "Studies in Christian Philosophy" (Macmillan). H. Rashdall, "Philosophy and Religion" (Scribners).

God. R. W. Micou, "Basic Ideas in Religion" (Association Press). C. A. Beckwith, "The Idea of God" (Macmillan). J. M. Shaw, "The Christian Doctrine of the Fatherhood of God" (Doran). Gore, "Belief in God" (Scribners).

Man and Evil. H. Wheeler Robinson, "The Christian Doctrine of Man" (Scribners). R. S. Moxon, "The Doctrine of Sin" (Doran). R. Mackintosh, "Christianity and Sin" (Scribners). E. Griffith-Jones, "Providence, Divine and Human," 2 vols. (Doran). W. E. Hocking, "Human Nature and Its Re-making," revised (Yale University).

Jesus Christ. C. Gore, "Belief in Christ" (Scribners). E. Lewis, "Jesus Christ and the Human Quest" (Abingdon Press). T. R. Glover, "Jesus in the Experience of Men" (Association Press). H. S. Coffin, "Portraits of Jesus Christ in the New Testament" (Macmillan).

The Christian Salvation. J. K. Mozley, "The Doctrine of Atonement" (Scribners). G. W. Richards, "Christian Ways of Salvation" (Macmillan). E. F. Scott, "The Spirit in the New Testament" (Doran).

The Future. W. A. Brown, "The Christian Hope" (Scribners). James Marchant, editor, "Immortality" (Putnam). S. D. F. Salmond, "The Christian Doctrine of Immortality" (Scribners). B. H. Streeter, editor, "Immortality" (Macmillan).

II

REFERENCE LITERATURE FOR EACH CHAPTER

The books most frequently referred to below have already been mentioned in the preceding bibliography, which gives author, title, and publisher. The name of the author only is repeated in these references. This should cause the student no confusion, since no more than one book is given by any one author. There are, however, a number of references given to books not mentioned in the bibliographies. The author, title, and publisher of these books are as follows.

A. C. Baird, "Christian Fundamentals" (Scribners). George Cross, "Creative Christianity" (Macmillan). H. R. Mackintosh, "Doctrine of the Person of Jesus Christ" (Scribners). J. H. Oldham, "Christianity and the Race Problem" (Doran). F. C. Platt, "Immanence and Christian Thought" (Abingdon Press). J. B. Pratt, "Matter and Spirit" (Macmillan). T. Rees, "The Holy Spirit" (Scribners). W. Sanday, "Christologies, Ancient and Modern" (Oxford University Press). George Steven, "The Psychology of the Christian Soul" (Doran).

Chapter I

Beckwith, chs. 2, 3, 11. Garvie, sec. II, ch. 1:1, ch. 2:1. Matthews, chs. 3, 6. Tillett, chs. 4, 8, 9. Lewis, ch. 4. Griffith-Jones, vol. I, bk. I, chs. 1, 2.

Chapter II

Beckwith, chs. 12, 13. Garvie, sec. II, chs. 2, 3. Matthews, ch. 2. Tillett, chs. 11, 15, 19. Shaw, ch. 1. Stevens, pt. I, ch. 6; pt. II, ch. 2; pt. VII, ch. 2.

Chapter III

Tillett, ch. 6. Stevens, pt. IV, chs. 2, 3. Garvie, sec. II, ch. 2. Rashdall, ch. 1. Griffith-Jones, vol. I, bk. II, chs. 1, 3. Pratt, chs. 1, 5. Hocking, pt. II, chs. 7, 8, 9, 10, 11, 12.

Chapter IV

Tillett, ch. 7. Clarke, pt. II, sec. 2. Rashdall, ch. 3. Edwards, ch. 3. Hocking, pt. III, chs. 13, 14, 15, 16. Platt, pt. IV, secs. 1, 2, 3, 4, 5.

Chapter V

Tillett, ch. 20 : 1. Garvie, sec. II, ch. 3. Brown, pt. IV, ch. 17. Griffith-Jones, vol. I, bk. III, chs. 1, 2. Lewis, chs. 5, 9. Stevens, pt. I, ch. 8; pt. II, ch. 3. Clarke, pt. III, sec. 3. Hocking, pt. III, chs. 17, 18, 19, 20.

Chapter VI

Garvie, sec. II, ch. 4 : 2. Clarke, pt. III, sec. 2, sec. 4. Stevens, pt. IV, chs. 4, 5. Griffith-Jones, vol. I, bk. II, ch. 2; bk. III, chs. 3, 4. Lewis, ch. 10. Richards, ch. 1. Moxon, ch. 7. Platt, pt. IV, secs. 7, 8, 9.

Chapter VII

Garvie, sec. I, ch. 1 : 1, ch. 2. Clarke, pt. IV, sec. I, 1, 2. Stevens, pt. I, chs. 4, 5. Lewis, chs. 7, 8, 18. Shaw, ch. 3. Richards, ch. 3. Gore, ch. 2. Coffin, chs. 3, 4, 5.

Chapter VIII

Tillett, ch. 17, secs. 1, 2. Garvie, sec. I, ch. 1 : 2, ch. 3, ch. 4 : 1, 3. Stevens, pt. II, ch. 4; pt. III, ch. 2; pt. IV, chs. 6, 7; pt. V, ch. 4; pt. VII, ch. 3. Lewis, ch. 19. Gore, chs. 3, 4, 7. Sanday, chs. 1, 2.

Chapter IX

Tillett, ch. 15. Garvie, sec. I, ch. 6. Clarke, pt. IV, sec. 4. Lewis, chs. 20, 21, 22, 23, 24. Shaw, ch. 4. Richards, chs. 11, 12. Glover, chs. 10, 11, 13. Baird, chs. 4, 5. Cross, ch. 2. Mackintosh, bk. III, pt. I, chs. 1, 2, 3.

Chapter X

Garvie, sec. III, ch. 1. Clarke, pt. V, secs. 1, 2, 3, 4, 5, 6. Stevens, pt. I, ch. 7; pt. II, ch. 5. Lewis, ch. 14. Scott, chs. 5, 6. Baird, ch. 10. Platt, pt. V, secs. 4, 5, 6. Rees, chs. 5, 6, 7, 8. Steven ("Psychology"), chs. 7, 8. Gore, "The Holy Spirit" (Scribners), ch. 4.

Chapter XI

Tillett, ch. 16. Garvie, sec. III, ch. 2. Lewis, ch. 1. Stevens, pt. I, chs. 3, 11; pt. IV, ch. 11; pt. VI, ch. 3. Shaw, chs. 5, 6. Richards, ch. 4. Baird, chs. 11, 12. Glover, chs. 9, 12. Oldham, chs. 14, 15, 16.

Chapter XII

Tillett, ch. 20 : 2. Garvie, sec. III, ch. 4. Clarke, pt. IV. Stevens, pt. I, ch. 12; pt. II, ch. 7; pt. IV, ch. 12; pt. VI, ch. 5. Lewis, ch. 25. Shaw, ch. 5. Baird, chs. 14, 15. Glover, ch. 7. Marchant, chs. 5, 8. Salmond, bk. VI, chs. 1, 2, 3, 4.

III

QUESTIONS FOR REVIEW

Chapter I

Give a general definition of the term God. Why do we need God in order to account for creation? In what way does the nature of man illustrate the nature of God? On what does religious experience rest? If all things reveal God, why may we still speak of degrees of divine revelation? In what three ways have men sought to relate God and the world? What difficulties arise from regarding God as entirely separate from the world? What difficulties arise from regarding God as completely identical with the world? What is meant by saying that God and the world are organically related? In what sense is God "within" the world? In what sense is God "without" the world?

Chapter II

State the chief characteristics of the Christian conception of God. Why may we believe that God is purposive? In what ways does life illustrate God's fatherly nature and purpose? What is meant by the statement that man's experience of God may be direct and immediate? What facts make intelligible and helpful the belief that God suffers? Why are God's love and God's holiness never in opposition? Why did the early church come to a belief in the Trinity? Why may we regard the idea of the Trinity as an attempt to express God's all-sufficiency? What assertions have Christian men made about God which cannot be supported from the mind of Christ? Why are we justified in rejecting all such assertions?

Chapter III

What may we infer from the fact that man has the native capacity to think about God? To what extent do the Scriptures support the view that man is both body and spirit?

What was the traditional Jewish and Christian belief as to the creation of man? What important differences in the Genesis narrative of creation did the traditional belief overlook? Does the scientific theory of man's continuity with the lower orders suffice to account for man's essential superiority? If not, how else can this superiority be accounted for? What may be said in criticism of the theory that spirit is simply a function of body? For what reasons is the human body to be reverenced rather than despised? Why must we include both body and mind in a complete description of personality? What difficulties go with this theory of double process?

CHAPTER IV

Why is man's moral nature not less significant, even if it is the result of a long and slow development? Why is it not less significant, even though to a large extent it is socially conditioned? Could a being not moral in itself ever be made moral by training? Why does the idea of "the better" always involve both a judging mind and a standard of judgment? What conditions are necessary to the activity of conscience? Is a moral judgment applied to the deed of another an act of conscience? Why must the standard of moral judgment continually change? Throughout this changing of standards, what remains unchangeable? What is meant by the social conscience? How is the social conscience related to the Kingdom of God?

CHAPTER V

Why does belief in the goodness of God intensify the problem of evil? What is meant by the statement that evil is relative rather than absolute? With reference to what do we judge evil? If evil is relative, does this mean that it is not real? Describe some of the forms of evil. Why may some evil be regarded as inevitable? To what extent may we regard some evil as avoidable? In which class of evils is sin to be included, and why? Is evil always punished? Is sin always punished? What distinction is to be made between punishment and suffering? When is punishment remedial? When is punishment retributive? Is punishment ever retributive only? Why could punishment alone never avail to win the sinner back?

Chapter VI

How can we account for moral evil without supposing demonic agency? In what sense is God involved in evil? Can he be involved in it without being wholly responsible for it? Is he also justified in judging it? Why are there evils that God does not prevent? If God's purpose with men renders evil inevitable, would it not have been better for him to change his purpose? Name some things that would become impossible if life were freed from all difficulty. What forms of evil does God oppose directly? What two particular forms does the opposition take? On what grounds may we believe that evil is a cause of divine suffering? Show that suffering may have redemptive significance.

Chapter VII

What are some of the differences in the written sources of our knowledge of Jesus Christ? Why may we depend on these sources? What facts justify Jesus being called Son of Man? What is the evidence to Jesus' profound religious faith? What did Jesus come to believe as to himself? In what sense was Jesus the embodiment of his own message? Why may we say that Jesus was greater in himself than anything he said or did? Why was the death of Jesus necessary to the completion of his testimony? Give the evidence that Jesus was a man of his own time. In what sense was Jesus a man of no time? What facts compel us to retain the element of mystery in our judgment of him?

Chapter VIII

Why had the early Christian thinkers a right to interpret the meaning Jesus had for them? Name the four factors in the interpretation. What was the history that the church interpreted? What place had experience in the interpretation, and what was this experience? What is meant by a world-view? Show that various New Testament writers all interpreted Jesus from the standpoint of their own world-view. In what sense did the Spirit guide the interpreters? What was the main problem of the successors of the Apostles? How did the Apostolic Fathers deal with this problem? How the Apologists? How the Alexandrian theologians? What did the Monarchians contend for? What formula was established at the Council of Nicæa? What divergent views continued to be expressed by Apollinaris, Nestorius, and Eutyches respectively? With these divergent views in mind, what pronouncement did the Council of Chalcedon make? What two fundamentals concerning Christ need to be preserved? In what sense is he Saviour? In what sense is he Lord?

CHAPTER IX

What factors help to perpetuate the traditional view of Christ? What are the real motives of those who are seeking to interpret Christ in a new way? What facts about the Gospel record are insisted on by criticism? In what sense was the making of creeds necessary? What objections may be offered to the phrase, "two natures in one person"? Why may we expect any formula concerning Christ to be eventually outgrown? What four facts are likely to be emphasized in the twentieth-century view of Jesus? Why ought we to ask how the human could seem divine rather than how the divine could become human? What truth did Jesus proclaim about God and man? How does Jesus' message "save"? Wherein resides the real authority of Jesus? What justifies us in distinguishing between the spirit of Jesus and the forms of its expression? How may we account for the differences between people? How does the principle that explains these differences also help to explain the uniqueness of Jesus Christ?

CHAPTER X

How did primitive people account for the ecstatic state? What things were ascribed to the Spirit in the Old Testament pre-prophetic period? What did the written prophets teach about the Spirit? What is the significance of the Psalter in this connection? What thought of the Spirit prevailed immediately before the coming of Christ? What do the Synoptic Gospels say about Jesus and the Spirit? What functions are assigned to the Spirit in the Acts? Explain the two types of teaching about the Spirit found in Paul. Also in the Fourth Gospel. Give the steps in the formulation of the church doctrine of the Spirit. What experiential facts lay at the root of the doctrine of the Holy Spirit? What would an attempt at re-interpreting the doctrine really aim to do? What two questions would the re-interpretation have to answer? What is meant by the Holy Spirit on its so-called objective side?

CHAPTER XI

In what sense did Jesus found the church? Why are we justified in saying that Jesus seemed not to be particularly interested in establishing an external organization? What are the significant features of the Christian brotherhood described in the early part of the Acts? What is the evidence in the Acts that this brotherhood soon began to develop ecclesiastical features? What conditions rendered this development necessary? Why ought we not to say that there is only one true form of church organization? What was Augustine's idea of the church? Why does excessive denominationalism not invalidate the Protestant principle? What justifies the distinction between the church and the churches? Why may we speak of a church outside the churches? What are the religious limitations on organizations which do Christian work, but are not themselves churches? What form may we expect Christianity to take as it becomes established in mission lands?

CHAPTER XII

In what respect was the early Hebrew interested in his future? What events led to the Hebrew interest in individual immortality? What place had the restored body in this Hebrew hope? Under what two forms has the teaching of Jesus respecting the future been preserved? Which form probably represents his real meaning? Show that the same two forms appear in the teaching of Paul. What is Paul's doctrine of the resurrection body? In what various ways have men answered the question whether immortality was for all alike? If all are at last to be saved, does that encourage moral indifference? Why is the choice between individual immortality and no immortality at all? Why, if we believe in Christ's eventual triumph, should we still struggle to make the present world-order Christian?

IV

RESEARCH TOPICS AND SUBJECTS

CHAPTER I

Religions and philosophies in which God is impersonal. Atheistic and theistic views of evolution. The different ways in which men have believed God makes himself known. Eternity of matter in Greek philosophy. The modern scientific theory of matter. The moral difficulties in pantheism. The sense in which God is "nearer" to some men than to others.

CHAPTER II

The reasons why science cannot speak the last word concerning God. The significance of man in view of the age and size of the universe. The meaning of the term "religious experience." The differences between faith and knowledge. Objections to the idea that God can suffer. The historical development of the doctrine of the Trinity. Old Testament assertions about God which the Christian must reject.

CHAPTER III

The different uses in the Scriptures of the word spirit. Reasons for questioning that God created instantly a fully developed human being. The various ways in which man "improves on nature." The psychological theories of parallelism, interactionism, and behaviorism. Examples of ascetic practices in religion. The body's control of the mind. The mind's control of the body.

CHAPTER IV

Changing ethical conceptions in the Scriptures; for example, revenge, punishment, and forgiveness. The possible relation between instinct and morality. Examples of practices once believed to be right, but now believed to be wrong. The possibility of a person being blameworthy, even although his conscience does not condemn him. The place of motive in the moral life. Forms of social wrong for which the individual may feel responsibility.

CHAPTER V

J. S. Mill's indictment of the equity of nature. The function of death in the natural order. Christian Science and the reality of evil. The conception of Satan. Theories of Utopia. Examples of remorse from literature. The meaning of "the sin against the Holy Ghost" as determined by the context of Matthew 12 : 22–37. Modern theories of criminal reform.

CHAPTER VI

Illustrations from human experience of good coming out of evil. The validity of the claim that God is infinitely sympathetic, but does not suffer. Possible limitations on the law of cause and effect. Sin as a disposition in distinction from sin as a particular deed. The sense in which selfishness is self-destruction. The part man must play in his own redemption.

CHAPTER VII

The theory that the Jesus of the Gospels is a composite mythical figure. Parables that are peculiar to Luke. The Passion Week in Matthew and John respectively. Temptations of Jesus other than the one immediately following his Baptism. The bearing of Jesus, prayer life on his humanness. Miracles of Jesus which cannot be explained by any known psychological laws. The distinction between Jesus as "timeless" and as "eternal." Theories of the method of Jesus' resurrection.

CHAPTER VIII

Some of the apparent differences between the Jesus of the Synoptic Gospels and the Christ of the Epistles. Peter's relation to the early church. The authorship of the Fourth Gospel. Evidences in Romans and Galatians of Paul's Jewish training. The Jewish sacrificial system and the Epistle to the Hebrews. The story of the Council of Nicæa. Differences between the School of Alexandria and the School of Antioch.

CHAPTER IX

The rights and the limitations of New Testament criticism. A comparative study of Acts 2 : 22–36 and Philippians 2 : 5–11.

The difference between "person" as used in the historic creeds, and "personality" as used to-day. Jesus' way of salvation in contrast to the ways prescribed by the various churches. Theories as to the seat of religious authority. The effect on the uniqueness of Jesus of surrendering belief in his virgin birth and his bodily resurrection. Ritschl's attempt to separate philosophy and theology.

CHAPTER X

The idea of inspiration in the light of psychology. The meaning of the prophetic formula: "The word of the Lord came unto me." The reform under Ezra and Nehemiah, and its effect upon the religious life of Israel. The varying accounts of the baptism of Jesus, and the meaning of the opening heavens, the voice, and the dove. "Speaking with tongues" in the New Testament. Causes of the division between the Eastern Church and the Western Church. The various means through which God approaches man.

CHAPTER XI

The various ways of interpreting Matthew 16 : 18. Theories of the Eucharist: Roman Catholic, Lutheran, Zwinglian. The meaning of "bishop" in the New Testament. The "love feast" (agape) in the early church. The Donatist theory of the church in contrast to the Augustinian. Advantages and disadvantages of one world-wide church. Defensible and indefensible conditions to church membership. The extent to which a church should engage in social and political activity.

CHAPTER XII

An interpretation of the description of the death of Elijah (II Kings 2 : 11, 12). Immortality in Egyptian thought. Immortality in Greek thought. The Roman Catholic doctrine of purgatory. The Protestant doctrine of an intermediate state. The meaning of Paul's words: "The last enemy that shall be destroyed is death" (1 Cor. 15 : 26). The reasons for and against the possibility of salvation after death. The extent to which one's estimate of the present life is affected by belief in immortality.

INDEX

149

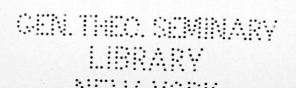

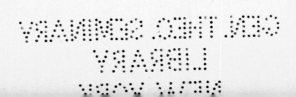